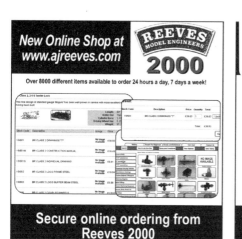

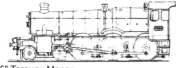
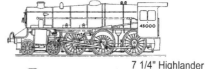

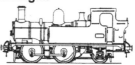
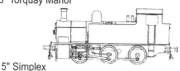

MODEL LOCOMOTIVE
VALVE GEARS

By **MARTIN EVANS**

TEE Publishing Ltd
The Fosse, Fosse Way
Leamington Spa
Warks. CV31 1XN

TEE
Publishing

Tel: 01926 614101
Fax: 01926 614293
E-mail: info@teepublishing.co.uk
W: www.teepublishing.co.uk

Published in England by
TEE Publishing Ltd.,
The Fosse, Fosse Way,
Nr. Leamington Spa,
Warks., CV31 1XN

For details of our other books visit:
www.teepublishing.co.uk

ISBN 1 85761 133 0
EAN 978 1 85761 133 5

Disclaimer:

Contents

Introduction

SINCE THE EARLIEST DAYS OF THE MODEL ENGINEERING MOVEMENT, the steam railway locomotive has always been the most popular prototype for builders of working models. Although steam traction on the railways of the world must now be regarded as obsolescent, the steam engine will be with us, with all its uncanny fascination, for many years yet. Even when that sad day is reached when the last steam locomotive makes its dismal journey to the scrapyard, the great hobby of constructing and operating model steam locomotives will go on with undiminished enthusiasm.

The cylinders and valve gear of the steam locomotive are probably the most important components of the whole machine. Were it not for the valves which distribute the steam to the cylinders, and the valve gear that controls them, a locomotive could not move at all. However large and efficient the boiler fitted, or however much high-pressure steam may be available, unless the valves and valve gear are properly designed and accurately fitted, the locomotive will be a failure.

An inefficient valve gear will not only reduce the power output and interfere with the smooth and free running of the engine, but it will also adversely affect the steaming qualities of the most efficient boiler, with the result that the design of the boiler may be wrongly blamed when the real trouble lies in the valve gear. Thus the cylinders, valves and valve gear must be correctly designed so as to make the best possible use of the steam produced by the boiler.

Although many fine designs of steam locomotive from Gauge O ($1\frac{1}{4}$ in.) to $10\frac{1}{4}$ in. gauge can be purchased, an increasing number of steam enthusiasts are now designing as well as building their own engines. Models of unusual types including narrow-gauge engines, Mallets, Garratts are being built. However, among these keen model engineers, there are some who, though fine craftsmen, are hazy on such subjects as the design of valve gears and the best proportions of cylinders and valves.

1

This new work attempts to help such people and, in its preparation, I have made use of the basic material in my previous book *Manual of Model Steam Locomotive Construction*. This has been carefully revised and added to, while the opportunity has been taken to include several additional types of valve gear, including some of the special types used with poppet valves. All the drawings have been revised, and many new ones included, in order that the various components for the different scales and gauges may be properly proportioned. To make this book as complete as possible, I have drawn upon the works of such well-known authorities as Mr. C. M. Keiller, Mr. K. N. Harris, "L.B.S.C.", the late J. N. Maskelyne, the late Henry Greenly, the late G. S. Willoughby, and the late C. S. Lake, whose articles have appeared from time to time in the pages of *Model Engineer*.

May I particularly commend to the attention of readers the chapter on poppet valves and valve gears, as these offer a field of experiment and development which, as far as model locomotives are concerned, is still wide open.

My thanks are due to British Railways, The New York Central Railroad Company, The Canadian Pacific Railway Company, the Société Nationale de Chemin de fer Francaise, and to Mr. B. Western of *Model Engineer* for many of the photographs.

If this short work proves of assistance to some of those fellow enthusiasts who are interested in this fascinating subject, I shall be well rewarded.

London.
June 1962.   MARTIN EVANS.

A good example of American-type Walschaerts' valve gear. An all-square layout with anchor link attached direct to crosshead.

[*Canadian Pacific Railway Company*

Rotary cam poppet valve gear, fitted to Gresley 3-cylinder 2-8-2.

[*British Railways*

[*British Railways*]

The Caprotti valve gear, as fitted to an ex-L.M.S. 4-6-0 of class 5 MT.

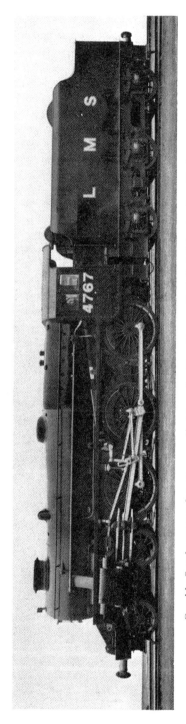

[*British Railways*]

Outside Stephenson valve gear applied to a double-chimney L.M.S. 4-6-0 mixed-traffic locomotive.

The Beames gear. This is basically a Walschaerts' gear used to operate valves situated between the frames but with the motion outside the frames.

[*British Railways*]

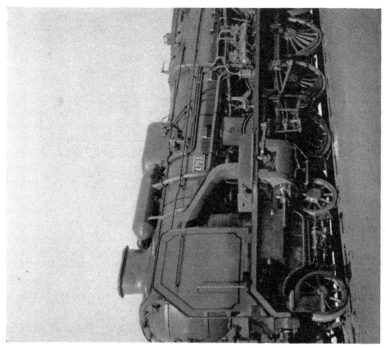

Oscillating cam poppet valve gear on French 4-8-0 compound.
[*Société Nationale de Chemin de Fer Francaise*

The Baker valve gear on a New York Central R.R. 4-6-4.
[*New York Central Railroad Company*

CHAPTER I

Basic proportions

AS THE ARRANGEMENT OF ANY LOCOMOTIVE VALVE GEAR DEPENDS directly on the proportions of the valves and ports in use, and as these again depend on the size and number of the cylinders, we should first examine these items in relation to the model locomotive under consideration.

General speaking, the model engineer will not go far wrong if he makes the cylinders to the scale dimensions of the prototype, or a shade smaller, though if the prototype was not a successful one in service, or had a reputation for being over- or under-cylindered, this recommendation will obviously be subject to modification. If it is desired to fit a boiler considerably over scale size (a practice which is

TABLE I

Recommended sizes of cylinders and ports

Gauge in.	Bore of cylinders in.	Stroke of cylinders in.	Steam ports. (slide valve) in.	Exhaust ports. in.	Piston valve dia. in.	Steam ports (piston valves) in.
$1\frac{1}{4}$	$\frac{5}{16}-\frac{3}{8}$	$\frac{9}{16}-\frac{5}{8}$	$\frac{1}{16} \times \frac{3}{16}$	$\frac{1}{8} \times \frac{3}{16}$	—	—
$1\frac{3}{4}$	$\frac{7}{16}-\frac{9}{16}$	$\frac{3}{4}-\frac{13}{16}$	$\frac{1}{16} \times \frac{5}{16}$	$\frac{1}{8} \times \frac{5}{16}$	$\frac{5}{16}$	$\frac{1}{16}$
$2\frac{1}{2}$	$\frac{11}{16}-\frac{7}{8}$	$1-1\frac{1}{2}$	$\frac{3}{32} \times \frac{1}{2}$	$\frac{3}{16} \times \frac{1}{2}$	$\frac{3}{8}-1$	$\frac{3}{32}$
$3\frac{1}{2}$	$1-1\frac{1}{4}$	$1\frac{1}{2}-1\frac{7}{8}$	$\frac{1}{8} \times \frac{13}{16}$	$\frac{9}{32} \times \frac{13}{16}$	$\frac{1}{2}-\frac{3}{4}$	$\frac{1}{8}$
5	$1\frac{1}{8}-1\frac{3}{4}$	$2\frac{1}{8}-2\frac{1}{2}$	$\frac{3}{16} \times 1$	$\frac{7}{16} \times 1$	$\frac{3}{4}-1$	$\frac{3}{16}$
$7\frac{1}{4}$	$2-2\frac{1}{2}$	$3\frac{1}{4}-3\frac{3}{4}$	$\frac{1}{4} \times 1\frac{1}{2}$	$\frac{9}{16} \times 1\frac{1}{2}$	$1-1\frac{3}{8}$	$\frac{1}{4}$
$9\frac{1}{2}$	$2\frac{3}{4}-3\frac{3}{8}$	$4-5$	$\frac{5}{16} \times 1\frac{7}{8}$	$\frac{11}{16} \times 1\frac{7}{8}$	$1\frac{1}{4}-1\frac{3}{4}$	$\frac{5}{16}$
$10\frac{1}{4}$	$3-3\frac{7}{8}$	$4\frac{3}{4}-5\frac{5}{8}$	$\frac{3}{8} \times 2\frac{1}{4}$	$\frac{13}{16} \times 2\frac{1}{4}$	$1\frac{1}{2}-2$	$\frac{3}{8}$
15	$3\frac{3}{4}-5$	$6-7\frac{1}{2}$	$\frac{1}{2} \times 3$	$1\frac{1}{8} \times 3$	$2-2\frac{5}{8}$	$\frac{1}{2}$

fortunately less common today), the cylinders could be a little larger than the scale dimensions would indicate.

In view of the fact that quite a number of free-lance models are constructed, it is thought that the foregoing table of suitable cylinder and port sizes may be helpful.

From the dimensions of the steam and exhaust ports we can obtain the dimensions of the valve.

The function of a valve, whether of the slide, piston, sleeve or poppet type, is to control the inlet of steam to the cylinders, and the outlet of it, after it has done its work on the piston, to the blast pipe.

TABLE II

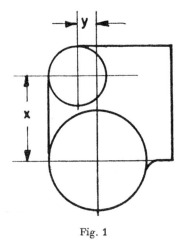

Fig. 1

Average heights and offsets of valve spindles for outside cylinders

Gauge in.	Height (x) in.	Offset (y) in.
$1\frac{3}{4}$	$\frac{11}{16}$	$\frac{5}{32}$
$2\frac{1}{2}$	$\frac{7}{8}$	$\frac{1}{4}$
$3\frac{1}{2}$	$1\frac{1}{4}$	$\frac{5}{16}$
5	$1\frac{3}{4}$	$\frac{7}{16}$
$7\frac{1}{4}$	$2\frac{3}{8}$	$\frac{5}{8}$
$9\frac{1}{2}$	$3\frac{1}{4}$	$\frac{3}{4}$
$10\frac{1}{4}$	$3\frac{5}{8}$	$\frac{13}{16}$
15	5	$1\frac{1}{4}$

There are four events which take place on each side of the piston during one revolution of the driving axle in the normal type of double-acting steam cylinder. These are:

1. Admission.
2. Cut off.
3. Exhaust.
4. Compression.

In normal running, admission of the steam takes place just before the piston reaches the end of its previous stroke. A small amount of the exhaust steam is trapped in the cylinder at the point of compression and between this point and the point of admission is the period of compression. Admission of live steam from the steam chest now takes place and raises the pressure in the cylinder to 80–90% of the boiler pressure. Steam then continues to enter the cylinder until the point of cut-off is reached, as determined by the valve gear, after which the steam continues to do work by expanding. When the piston has nearly reached the end of its stroke, the valve opens to exhaust, and the period of exhaust takes place until the valve closes to exhaust, and the point of compression occurs.

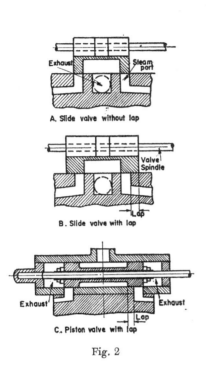

A. Slide valve without lap

B. Slide valve with lap

C. Piston valve with lap

Fig. 2

Lap and Lead

The lap and lead of a steam engine valve are two dimensions of vital importance, and the reason for their use often baffles the beginner.

During the early days of the steam locomotive, the slide valves used were not provided with lap, i.e. the valves just spanned the ports, thus at almost any position the valve was either open to live steam or to exhaust, and the steam was, of course, used most wastefully as it had no chance to expand. In modern engines, lap is added to the valve, allowing early cut-off and "expansive" working, and giving smooth and economical running as described previously in the cycle of valve events.

The lap of a valve may be defined as the amount by which the valve overlaps the outside edge of the steam port when the valve is in its mid position.

In a steam engine cylinder where no lead has been given to the valve, when the piston is exactly on dead centre, the valve is just about to open the port to the live steam at that end. If the valve opens to steam before the piston reaches dead centre, it is said to have lead.

Lead may therefore be defined as the amount by which the valve has opened the port to live steam when the main crank is at the dead centre position.

In full-size locomotive work, a certain amount of lead is essential for fast running, though the amount which should be provided, in relation to the other factors involved, has always been a matter of acute controversy among locomotive engineers. To complicate matters, some valve gears provide a constant lead, whatever the position of the driver's reversing lever, while other gears, such as Stephenson's, give differing leads according to the position of the die block in the expansion link.

It is not possible to state what would be the ideal amount of lead to provide for a given size of cylinder as this depends on so many other factors, such as the lap of the valves, the port width, the cross-sectional area of the regulator port, superheaters, steam pipes and steam passages in the cylinder itself, the cylinder clearance volume, the piston-swept volume, and of course the type of valve gear in use. Then again the draughting arrangements also have a bearing on the matter.

As regards the three main factors involved in the valve itself, i.e. lap, lead, and valve travel, increasing the lead while keeping the other two items constant, in addition to giving earlier admission of the steam, gives an earlier cut-off, an earlier release to exhaust, and increased compression.

Lap and Lead for model cylinders

Generally speaking, the lap of the valves in model cylinders, with a valve gear such as Stephenson's, Joy's, Walschaerts' or Baker's, should be made between three-quarters and the full size of the port width.

The lead, in the case of constant lead valve gears such as Joy's, Walschaerts' or Baker's, should be made between $\frac{1}{9}$ and $\frac{1}{13}$ of the lap. Where a valve gear such as Stephenson's is used, a variable lead is produced, and the gear should be so designed as to give the required lead at about 30% cut-off. This will be discussed in a later chapter.

To ensure the locomotive having a free exhaust, some designers give "exhaust clearance" to the valves. Exhaust clearance can be defined as the amount by which the inside edges of the valve overlap the inside edges of the steam ports, or in other words, the amount by which the valve is open to exhaust when in its mid position. If exhaust clearance is given, the release of the steam from the cylinder occurs earlier; at the same time, the closing of the exhaust port occurs later.

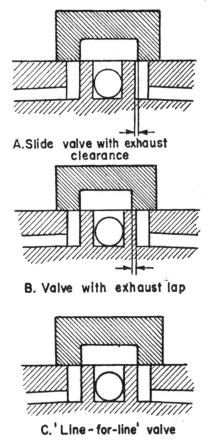

A. Slide valve with exhaust clearance

B. Valve with exhaust lap

C. 'Line-for-line' valve

Fig. 3 *Slide valves to show exhaust clearance*

Of course, a valve could also be given the opposite of exhaust clearance, generally called "exhaust lap", but as this would cause a late release of the exhaust steam, it is seldom used. For all-round performance and with ample steam pipes and passages, the line-for-line arrangement is sound practice—i.e. the distance between the inside edges of the valve is the same as that between the inside edges of the steam ports. If exhaust clearance is used, it should not amount to more than $\frac{1}{2}$–$\frac{3}{4}$ of the lead.

The steam passageways between the bores of the cylinders and the ports should be made of reasonable size and as direct as possible. In large model locomotives with slide valves, the total cross-sectional area of the passageway may be made nearly as great as the area of the steam ports, thus when the locomotive is being worked at short cutoffs, there will be no throttling of the exhaust steam.

It must not be forgotten that, in all normal steam cylinders, the steam passageways are also acting as exhaust ways.

Although the streamlining of the steam pipes is not likely to have much effect on the performance of small models, attention should always be given to the exhaust arrangements, the exhaust pipes being of ample cross-sectional area and as direct as possible. The blast nozzle too should be properly shaped and correctly aligned in relation to the chimney and petticoat pipe.

Valve travel

In a two-cylinder locomotive, the cut-off in full gear should not be made too early, otherwise starting with a load or on a gradient will be difficult. About 80% is a good average figure, while 3-cylinder locomotives with the main cranks at 120 deg. should have a full gear cut-off of at least 75% for the best results. As a matter of fact, anything up to 85% is of advantage in starting; beyond that figure, the angle which the main crank makes with the longitudinal centreline of the motion is too small for the push from the piston to have much effect. In practice, the limitation of full gear cut-off is generally a mechanical one, in that sufficient room cannot be found for a valve gear giving the valve travel necessary.

If the valve opens the ports fully in full gear, the valve travel will be twice the port-width-plus-lap in full gear.

The cut-off in full gear can be calculated as follows:

$$\text{Cut-off} = \frac{\text{port}^2 + 2(\text{port} \times \text{lap})}{(\text{port} + \text{lap})^2} \times 100\%$$

To take some examples, if the port width in a model cylinder is say $\frac{1}{8}$ in., and the lap is $\frac{3}{32}$ in., then:

$$\text{Cut-off} = \frac{\frac{1}{8}^2 + 2(\frac{1}{8} \times \frac{3}{32})}{(\frac{1}{8} + \frac{3}{32})^2} \times 100\%$$
$$= 82\% \text{ approx.}$$

If the port width is say $\frac{1}{4}$ in., and the lap $\frac{1}{4}$ in., then:

$$\text{Cut-off} = \frac{\frac{1}{4}^2 + 2(\frac{1}{4} \times \frac{1}{4})}{(\frac{1}{4} + \frac{1}{4})^2} \times 100\%$$
$$= 75\% \text{ approx.}$$

In the above formula, lead is neglected, but this would decrease the cut-off point.

CHAPTER II

Single-eccentric and slip-eccentric gears

THE MOST SIMPLE FORM OF VALVE GEAR IS THE SINGLE ECCENTRIC motion. This valve gear is not reversible and is thus unsuitable for locomotives. However, the movement of the valve given by this motion enables us better to understand the more complicated valve gears such as Stephenson's.

The setting of a single eccentric driving a valve without lap is always exactly 90 deg. in advance of its crankpin. When the valve is

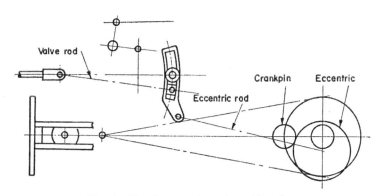

Fig. 4 *Simple-eccentric motion without lap*

provided with lap, or with lap and lead, the eccentric must be further advanced by that amount. It is important to note that the angle of advance of an eccentric is the angle it is moved *ahead* of the normal 90 deg.

9

Slip eccentric valve Gear

The only really simple reversing valve gear is probably the slip-eccentric gear. This gear gives a good steam distribution especially if the eccentric rod is long, though no adjustment of cut-off is possible, nor can the engine so fitted be reversed from the cab without much complication (such as a gear and ratchet mechanism operating on the crankshaft). However as much lap and lead as is desired can be applied and a cut-off suitable for continuous running chosen.

The slip-eccentric gear has been used in full-size practice on occasion, a notable example being the Webb 3-cylinder compound engines of the old L.N.W.R., in which this gear was adopted for operating the valve of the low-pressure cylinder.

The eccentric is arranged loose upon the axle and is driven by a stud or pin mounted in a collar which is secured to the axle alongside the eccentric. Alternatively, the pin is attached to the eccentric and is driven by a suitably shaped collar.

The slip eccentric gear is ideal for simple steam models of $1\frac{1}{4}$ in. and $1\frac{3}{4}$ in. gauge, which are generally run on scenic model railways and not used for passenger hauling. The valve travel should be made rather less than what would be used on a passenger-hauling locomotive. A good all-round figure would be three-quarters the amount of valve travel normally allowed in full gear.

For instance, for a locomotive having $\frac{3}{32}$ in. wide steam ports and a lap of $\frac{3}{32}$ in., the valve travel would be made:

$$\frac{3}{4} \times 2(\tfrac{3}{32} + \tfrac{3}{32}) \text{ in.}$$
$$= \tfrac{9}{32} \text{ in.}$$

Thus the throw of the eccentric in this example would amount to $\frac{9}{64}$ in.

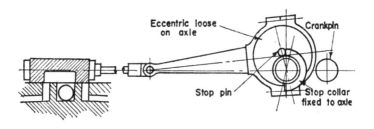

Fig. 5   *Slip-eccentric valve gear*

TABLE III

Recommended Valve Travels and Eccentric Throws for Slip Eccentric
Valve Gear (inches)

	Steam Ports	Lap	Valve travel	Eccentric throw
Gauge 0	$\frac{1}{16} \times \frac{3}{16}$	·050	·171	·0855
Gauge 1	$\frac{1}{16} \times \frac{5}{16}$	·063	·1875	·094
$2\frac{1}{2}$ in. gauge	$\frac{3}{32} \times \frac{5}{8}$	·094	$\frac{9}{32}$	$\frac{9}{64}$

CHAPTER III

The Stephenson link valve gear

VALVE GEARS WHICH CAN BE CONTROLLED FROM THE CAB, ALLOWING the engine to be reversed as required, and the cut-off adjusted as needed to cope with the condition of the road and the load behind the tender, can be divided into three main classes: Link motions, radial valve gears, and poppet valve gears.

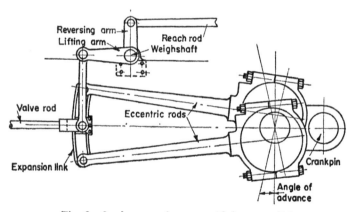

Fig. 6 *Stephenson valve gear with loco-type link*

The principal link motions are the Stephenson, the Gooch and the Allan straight-link.

The Stephenson valve gear takes its name from the famous firm of Robert Stephenson and Company. It was not actually invented by Robert Stephenson himself, but was evolved by the company about 1843. Who first thought of the idea is not quite clear; probably William Williams, an apprentice draughtsman at Newcastle, first had the idea, but William Howe, one of the pattern makers employed by the company, worked out the practical details. At all events, the gear proved a great improvement on the clumsy "gab" gear previously used, and with various detail improvements, the Stephenson gear has been used in all types of steam engine ever since.

The Stephenson link valve gear was at one time the most widely used locomotive valve gear in Great Britain, though it has now been very largely superseded by the Walschaerts', the Baker gear, and the various types of poppet valve gear. It is still however a very efficient valve gear if properly designed.

The Stephenson gear uses two eccentrics, one for each direction of working, the eccentrics being generally mounted on the driving axle. The eccentric rods are connected to each end of a curved slotted expansion link, arranged so as to lie with its concave side towards the driving axle. In the "locomotive type" link, the eccentric rods are connected on the curved centre-line of the link, above and below the link slot, thus the total travel of the eccentrics is made more than the valve travel required in full gear.

The locomotive type link is generally suspended at its centre point by means of a bracket attached to it, carrying a pin upon which works a lifting link which is connected by an arm to the weighshaft. The valve rod usually works in a guide attached to the motion plate, or it may be operated by a link attached to a swinging lever, pivoted to some convenient point on the mainframes. The valve rod obtains its motion from a die-block, upon which the curved slot of the expansion link can slide up and down as controlled by the reversing lever through the weighshaft, lifting arm and lifting link.

On six and eight coupled locomotives, the eccentric rods are some-

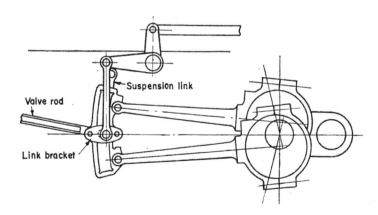

Fig. 7   *Stephenson valve gear with Launch-type link*

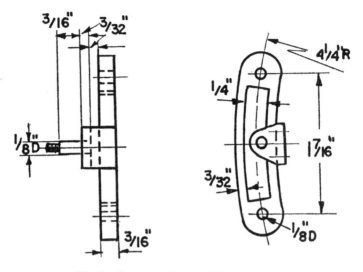

Fig. 8   *Loco-type link for ¾ in. scale engine*

times made very long and set over in order to clear the axle ahead of the driving axle.

Although a direct drive, parallel with the horizontal centre-line of the motion, is desirable with Stephenson gear, if the valves are on top of the cylinders, or below, direct drive inclined to the cylinders is equally satisfactory, although in the case of slide valve cylinders, the port face of the cylinder block has to be machined off at a suitable angle. In the case of piston valve cylinders, careful setting-up is necessary, to ensure boring the block for the valve at the correct angle.

Sometimes an indirect drive is used with Stephenson valve gear, a rocking shaft being adopted, working in bearings attached to the mainframes. While this is quite satisfactory, care must be taken in fitting the various pins, otherwise lost motion will spoil the efficiency of the gear.

An interesting and very useful feature of the Stephenson valve gear is that with "open" eccentric rods, the lead increases towards mid-gear. This is due to the angularity of the rods and the effect is greater the shorter the eccentric rods. If "crossed" eccentric rods are used, the lead would decrease towards mid-gear, an undesirable feature in a railway locomotive.

Another type of Stephenson gear is that where the expansion link used is the "Launch-type" link. The true Launch link has the point

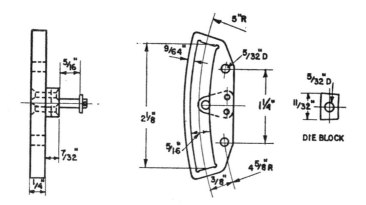

Fig. 9   *Launch-type link for 5 in. gauge model*

of suspension on the curved centre-line of the link slot but beyond one end of the slot, but in the Launch-type link, the suspension is arranged on the horizontal centre-line of the motion.

Alexander Allan, of the L.N.W.R., was probably the first engineer to realise the possibilities of the Launch-type link with Stephenson's valve gear, but it was G. J. Churchward of the old Great Western Railway who developed this type of gear to its present high efficiency, by adapting it for the use of large laps and long valve travels.

About the year 1904, Churchward adopted long valve travels and large steam laps for his express locomotives; he soon realised however that if he was to use the usual locomotive type link, the length of link required and the large size of eccentric sheaves and straps needed, would make the arrangement quite impracticable in the space available. He therefore adopted the Launch-type link with comparatively short eccentric rods and, as the latter gave a large increase of lead towards mid-gear, he arranged for the valves to be set with negative lead in full-gear, i.e. the valve did not open to steam until the piston had passed dead centre.

This negative lead would appear to have confused many model engineers, but it should be understood that the negative lead in itself was not necessarily desired, but with the short eccentric rods used, if the valves had been set "line-for-line", there would have been excessive lead when the engine was notched up for fast running.

In fact it was found that on the Great Western, this negative full-gear lead did not adversely affect starting or acceleration. Such engines as the 4-6-0 Saints and Halls fitted with this type of gear were excellent starters. In any case as soon as the driver had his train well under way, he would start to notch up his reversing gear, and the negative lead would soon change to a positive one.

Stephenson valve gear outside the frames

Although Stephenson valve gear is nearly always arranged inside the frames of the locomotive, there is no reason why it should not be placed outside the frames, to operate the valves of the typical outside type of cylinder with valves on top.

One of the Stanier 4-6-0 class 5's, No. 4767, was fitted with a type of Stephenson valve gear, resembling the Churchward arrangement, outside the frames. The launch-type link was centre-suspended, and the valve rod was carried at the rear end by a long suspension lever just ahead of the link, and at the front end by a similar though shorter lever. Instead of the eccentrics used in the more conventional type of Stephenson gear, two cranks were arranged, attached to the main crankpin. The whole assembly was neat and unobtrusive, yet all parts were extremely accessible for maintenance purposes. This type of gear could be used on models with success provided that the main crankpin was made stout enough to carry the extra load, especially if slide valves were contemplated.

Designing Stephenson's link valve gear for models

Before the proportions of the components of the valve gear itself can be considered, the full gear cut-off should be decided upon.

In full-size locomotive work, the point of cut-off in full gear is usually decided by the class of work the engine is required to perform. A two-cylinder contractors' type of shunting locomotive would proably be given a full gear cut-off of at least 85% of the stroke, a shunting or goods engine 80 to 85%, while an express passenger locomotive would be given about 75% if a two-cylinder machine, possibly less if a three-cylinder, with cranks at 120 deg. The express engine would not of course be required to start and stop nearly so frequently as the shunting or goods engine, nor would the maximum load to be hauled be so great in relation to the theoretical tractive effort of the locomotive, thus an earlier cut-off could be used.

In the case of model locomotives, which may be used equally on a fast continuous track or on a short up and down line, it is advisable to make the full gear cut-off fairly late. It is of course true that at late cut-offs the angle of the connecting rod in relation to the main crank is very small; even so, it may be taken that anything up to 85% cut-off is useful in starting a two-cylinder locomotive. In any case, provided that the mechanical layout allows for it and that there is sufficient clearance for the various parts, there are no disadvantages attending the use of a late cut-off in full gear. There are however two distinct advantages: one is that a late cut-off gives full steam port opening early in the stroke; the other is that a locomotive so arranged has a more even turning movement at slow speeds, so that the tendency to slip at starting is reduced.

To obtain a full gear cut-off of 80% of the stroke, the full gear valve travel should be made $4\frac{1}{2}$ times the lap of the valve; for 85%, the full gear travel should be 5 times the lap. This of course ignores any lead that may be given to the valve, but with launch-type links with comparatively short eccentric rods, the valves should have no lead at all in full gear, but should be set line-for-line with the outside edges of the steam ports, with the cranks on dead centre. With locomotive type links and long eccentric rods, a small amount of full gear lead may be allowed for, and this would make the cut-off earlier.

Proportions of Stephenson's valve gear

If success is to be achieved, the various parts of Stephenson's gear must be carefully proportioned and the following dimensions, evolved from highly successful working models, may be relied upon:

1. Throw of eccentrics (for Launch-type links) = $\frac{1}{2}$ full gear valve travel.

2. Thickness of eccentric straps should be between $\frac{1}{5}$ and $\frac{1}{6}$ of piston diameter, to the nearest round figure.

3. Motion pins should be approximately $\frac{1}{8}$ of piston diameter.

4. Boss diameters on links, eccentric rods and valve rods = twice motion pin diameter.

5. Width of curved slot of expansion link = pin diameter $\times 1\frac{3}{4}$ approx.

6. Thickness of expansion link should be between $\frac{1}{5}$ and $\frac{1}{7}$ of piston diameter, according to space available.

7. Distance between eccentric rod pins should be full gear valve travel multiplied by 2 for short eccentric rods, or by $2\frac{1}{8}$ for long eccentric rods (by short rods is meant rods of a scale equivalent of less than 4 ft. 6 in.)

8. Length of curved slot in link should be eccentric rod pin centres ×
1⅝.

9. Length of die-block = motion pin diameter × 2⅛ to the nearest
round figure.

The point of suspension of the expansion link

The point of suspension of the expansion link in Stephenson's gear
makes a great deal of difference to the valve events obtained. On
some models, the lifting link is attached to one of the eccentric rod
pins. However, this is not good practice, and is only done to avoid the
extra work involved in arranging a proper central suspension; it can
only lead to unequal valve events.

In locomotives fitted with the Stephenson's link motion, it is very
important that the eccentric sheaves and eccentric rods should be so
fitted up that the engine has "open" eccentric rods, enabling the lead
to increase towards mid gear. To ensure that this is so, the right-
hand motion of the model should be drawn out, in as large a scale as
possible, with the right hand crankpin on the back dead-centre. Then
the outside eccentric rod nearest to the right-hand mainframe is the
forward one, and is connected to the top boss of the expansion link.
The inside eccentric rod is the backward one, and is connected to the
bottom boss of the expansion link.

In this position, the forward eccentric will be up, and the backward
eccentric down, and the expansion link will stand exactly vertical to
the horizontal centre-line of the motion. The lifting link should now
lie quite vertical and from this the correct position for the weighshaft
may be decided.

If the valve gear actuates the valves through the medium of a
rocking shaft, the eccentric rods are connected as described previously,
but the eccentric sheaves are set exactly opposite to the previous
position with the crankpin on back dead-centre. This means that the
forward eccentric sheave is now down and the backward sheave is up,
and the eccentric rods are therefore crossed at this position of the
crankpin.

In order to arrive at the best possible position for the suspension
of the expansion link by the lifting links where long valve travels are
required, it is necessary to consider what errors, caused by the
obliquity of the link when fully inclined forward or backward, have to
be neutralised. With the Launch-type link, there are two main kinds
of "link-slip", therefore the point of suspension of the link must be

chosen such that each of these two kinds of link-slip is not decreased at the expense of an increase in the other.

By suspending the expansion link on its horizontal centre-line, certain advantages are gained. Firstly the suspension point is never very far away from the die-block in any position of the gear, so that the lifting links always have a good leverage to hold the link with a minimum of link-slip. Secondly the steam distribution improves, and link-slip decreases, as the valve gear is "notched up" towards mid gear, as this

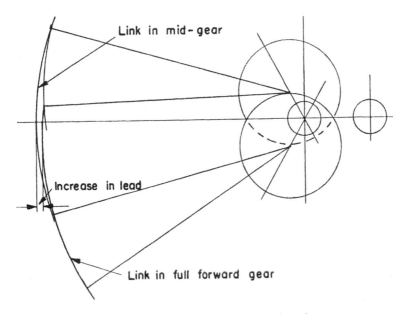

Fig. 10   *Showing increase in lead towards mid gear*

brings the suspension centre still closer to the die-block. Also as the suspension centre is midway along the link, the steam distribution will be equally good in forward or backward gear.

Another advantage of suspending the expansion link on its horizontal centre-line is that the swing of the lifting link is very small; this of course reduces wear, but more important it means that there is very little swinging effect transmitted from the lifting links to the expansion link itself, which would otherwise tend to move the link vertically up and down on the die-block.

It is now necessary to decide upon what point, on this horizontal centre-line, to locate the pins for the lifting links. If the expansion link is suspended at the point where this horizontal centre-line cuts the curved centre-line of the link slot, it will be found that this position allows of rather too much link-slip owing to the fact that this point of suspension is too far forward from the points from which the expansion link is driven, i.e. the eccentric rod pins. The eccentric rods have less control over the action of the link at the position where the die-block is located, and thus allow the link to rise and fall upon the die-block to some extent, making the cut-off earlier at one end of the cylinder than at the other.

If the expansion link is suspended at the point where a line drawn between the two eccentric rod pins crosses the horizontal centre-line, it is found that the lifting links do not swing so much during the movement of the expansion link as they are now pivoted on a neutral centre. However it is also found that the rocking action of the eccentric rods is now transmitted to the expansion link in a more marked degree, thus introducing a more severe link-slip, the expansion link sliding up and down the die-block to some extent, giving a faulty steam distribution.

It will now be apparent that the position for the attachment of the lifting links should lie between these two positions and rather nearer to the former. The ideal position depends finally upon the proportionate length of the eccentric rods. With short eccentric rods, the second or more virulent error is likely and therefore the point of suspension may be further forward, i.e. nearer to the curved centre-line of the link slot; if a line is drawn between the centres of the two die-block positions in full forward and backward gear respectively, this may be taken as the most *forward* position advisable, while for long eccentric rods (i.e. rods of a scale length of 5 ft. or over) the most *backward* position advisable may be taken as the point where the horizontal centre-line cuts the rear edge of the curved slot in the link.

When space permits, two lifting links may be used, one on each side of the expansion link, and suitable brackets should be riveted to the link to carry them, with the necessary clearance for the valve rod fork to embrace the die-block.

It is most important in Stephenson valve gear, and in fact in other link valve gears, that all the eccentric rods are made exactly the same length, otherwise serious errors in the steam distribution may be caused. To avoid this, some form of jig should be made up. A suitable jig might consist of a length of flat steel bar of convenient dimensions on which is set out the overall length of the eccentric rods as accurately as possible; a silver-steel peg is then pressed in at one end, this peg being made a close fit in the eccentric rod forks; at the other end, a circular disc, turned to exactly the same diameter as the eccentric sheaves in use, is fitted, the disc being shouldered down and pressed into the jig. When each complete eccentric rod and strap will fit on such a jig, they will be relatively the same length to quite fine limits.

It is also important that the lifting links are made exactly the same length, though this can be accomplished very easily by drilling the two components together. The lifting arms, which are attached to the weighshaft, must be arranged exactly parallel to each other and in the mid gear position should be parallel to the longitudinal centre-line of the motion. The reversing arm, which is connected to the cab reversing gear by the reach rod, is generally, but not necessarily, arranged at right angles to the lifting arms.

Full gear lead

When setting the valves of a Stephenson valve gear, the problem always arises of how much lead to allow the valve in full gear. As was mentioned earlier, with the normal arrangement of "open" eccentric rods, the lead increases towards mid gear. The amount of this increase may be calculated as follows:

$$\text{Increase in lead} = \frac{c \times t \cos A}{l}$$

where $c = \frac{1}{2}$ the distance between eccentric rod pins.

l = length of eccentric rod.

t = throw of eccentric.

A = angle of advance.

It will thus be seen that the length of the eccentric rods as well as the lap of the valves has an important bearing on the matter. With long lap valves and comparatively short eccentric rods, the valves should be set with no lead at all in full gear. It might be thought that this arrangement would give an engine lacking in accelerative powers, but if the engine is driven in the proper manner, starting off in full gear with the regulator just open, followed by a reduction in cut-off and an increase in regulator opening as the train gathers speed, the best results will be obtained.

If long eccentric rods are in use, the increase of lead towards mid gear will be less, and therefore some full gear lead may be given, especially in the smaller scales, though it should only be a small amount. As there are so many variable factors which have a bearing on the matter, it is difficult to advise an exact figure, but an amount equal to $\frac{1}{10}$ or $\frac{1}{12}$ of the lap will generally be found satisfactory.

Construction of Stephenson's valve gear

The expansion links are probably the most important components in the valve gear, and care in their manufacture is always well rewarded. The ideal material to use is probably "gauge plate" (ground carbon water or oil-hardening steel) which can be hardened before final assembly. Bright mild steel of good quality, suitably case-hardened, makes quite a good substitute, and is more easily worked. Though stainless steel is sometimes used, the difficulty of machining some grades of stainless steel may deter most builders from using this material.

The curved slot should be carefully marked out, cut and finished to size and the eccentric rod pin holes drilled and reamed before the outside of the link is cut to shape. Although the curved slot can be finished by hand, using the die-block, which is previously made, as a gauge, the best results are generally obtained by some form of machine operation. If a vertical milling machine is available, the set-up for machining this slot is quite a simple one. For those who must use the centre lathe, some means must be provided for swinging the link blank on a pin at the required radius, the actual machining being done by means of a small end-mill or slot-drill in the chuck or collet.

A useful milling attachment for machining links in the lathe is shown in Plate facing page 91. A stout steel bar is clamped horizontally in a machine vice bolted to the vertical slide; the link blank, with two links marked out and pivot holes drilled and reamed at the correct radius, is bolted to the bar by means of a nut and fibre washer, and is traversed about the pivot bolt by means of the screw, nut and connecting link seen. The fibre washer helps to prevent snatch as the cutter is engaged. To reduce the work actually done by the cutter, a double row of holes may first be drilled on the line of the curved slot and the unwanted piece broken out.

A milling attachment of this type is suitable for expansion links of quite a wide difference in radii, the limitation being excessive angularity between the curved arc described by the link blank and the connecting lever. Care should be taken when making an attachment of this type to ensure that the link blank is reamed a good fit on the pivot bolt, otherwise chatter may be experienced.

Another method of milling expansion links is by bolting the link to the lathe faceplate at the required distance out from the mandrel centre and using a milling spindle bolted to the cross-slide or top-slide. Although on small lathes, this method may result in the link blank overhanging the faceplate, this is not a disadvantage up to a point, especially if the blank is a stout one. The bar used for the expansion link can in fact be made considerably longer to give a hand grip, the bar being swung by hand against the rotation of the end-mill in the milling spindle.

After the expansion links have been hardened, they should be checked very carefully for distortion. In the case of mild-steel case-hardened links, it is usually a simple matter to correct any such distortion by bending.

Although milling can also be resorted to for the production of the link die-blocks, in the smaller scales the work of setting up may not be considered justified, and careful filing should prove satisfactory. In larger scales, the die-blocks could be end-milled in a similar manner to the link slots. The die-blocks should be hardened right out.

When the links and die-blocks are ready, the link brackets, by which the links are suspended, are made up and fitted. It is not essential to fit brackets to both sides of the link provided that the length of the bearing of the lifting link on its pin is not less than twice the diameter of the lifting link pin.

The link brackets are generally made of mild steel, case-hardened, and riveted to the link in such a manner as to allow working clearance for the intermediate valve spindle or valve rod jaw, and the die-block pin which passes through this. Where link brackets are fitted to both sides of the link, great care should be taken to ensure that these are exactly in line and level with each other.

The making of the eccentric rods should present no particular difficulties, mild steel with case-hardened or bronze-bushed eyes being generally used. The holes for the eccentric rod pins should be drilled first, and the slot for the link cut by means of a small face cutter mounted between centres or on a stout arbor in the chuck or collet. The eccentric straps, which are generally gunmetal or phos-bronze castings, are machined to suit the eccentric sheaves before attaching to the eccentric rods. It is generally advisable to drill and tap for the securing bolts before sawing the two halves apart, after which the jointing faces can be finished and the halves bolted together again temporarily and set up in the four-jaw chuck for boring the inside.

A short length of steel bar, previously turned to exactly the same diameter as the eccentric sheaves, may be used as a gauge when boring the straps, this bar can then be used to hold the straps while the sides of the latter are machined. The screws are slackened off and a strip of paper put between the straps and the bar; on re-tightening, the straps will be firm enough to enable light cuts to be taken across each side.

Before fitting the eccentric straps to their rods, an assembly jig should be made up as described in a previous paragraph. There are two generally accepted methods of fitting the rods to the straps. One is by slotting the strap, inserting the end of the rod and riveting through the two; the other, used in larger models, is to form a head on the eccentric rod and to fit studs to the strap for bolting the two together.

The weighshaft, which should be of stout construction, may be carried in gunmetal bushes into, or bolted to the mainframes, and the lifting arms and reversing arm can be held to the weighshaft by means of taper pins through their bosses.

The valve spindles must always be made adjustable for length, unless adjustment can be carried out between the valve and the valve spindle. The valve spindles should work through a regular packed gland, and a tail-guide on the front end of the steam chests helps to prevent the valve spindles from sagging and keeps the valves square with the ports.

In full-size practice it is usual to fit balance weights or springs to the weighshaft of the Stephenson valve gear, to lighten the load on the reversing gear, but this is not necessary on models below 3 in. scale.

CHAPTER IV

The Gooch, and Allan straight-link valve gears

THE GOOCH OR STATIONARY LINK MOTION BEARS SOME RESEMBLANCE to the Stephenson gear, as two eccentrics mounted on the driving axle are used, but the expansion link is hung from its centre point and is not raised or lowered by means of the reversing lever; the link is also arranged with its concave side towards the cylinder end of the motion.

The valve or radius rod is raised and lowered by a lifting link attached to the weighshaft, thus reversing the engine or altering the cut-off in the usual way. The expansion link itself is usually of the box type, consisting of two curved channels, of radius equal to the length of the radius rod, placed facing one another, distance pieces being inserted at each end. The expansion link is hung from fairly long suspension links, so that the rise of the link at each end of its swing shall cause the least interfence with its proper movement. As the radius of the expansion link is equal to the length of the radius rod, when the crank is at dead-centre and the port open to lead steam, reversing the motion simply lifts or lowers the radius rod and does not move the valve; thus the lead is constant for all positions of the reversing lever and open or crossed eccentric rods can be employed without affecting its peculiarities.

To minimise the slip of the die-block in the link, from which this valve gear is liable to suffer if allowed to get slack and worn, it is usual to modify the method of setting so as to make the distribution of steam more nearly correct in forward gear, at the expense to some extent of backward gear, and in practice this is done by suspending the expansion link with its centre just below the centre-line of the motion, the back gear eccentric rod being lengthened and the angle of advance of the back gear eccentric reduced to suit. Die-slip cannot be entirely eliminated as the radius rod has not the power to hold

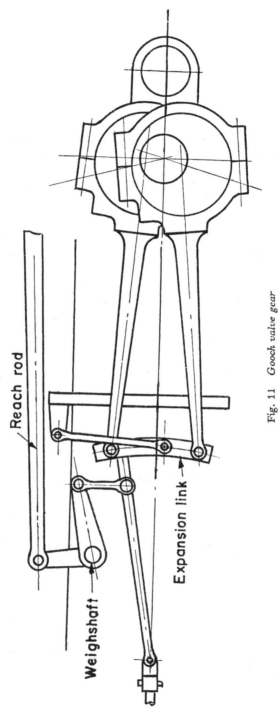

Reach rod

Expansion link

Weighshaft

Fig. 11 Gooch valve gear

Reidinger rotary poppet valve gear fitted to London Midland Region 2-6-0 class 5, No. 42825.

[British Railways

Part of the outside motion of a rebuilt Southern Pacific. The valve spindle receives its motion via a suspension link and the cylinders are of the outside admission type.

Typical of British Railways practice, the outside Walschaerts' gear fitted to standard class 5 locomotive.

the die-block with the same vertical rigidity as the valve spindle guides often employed with Stephenson's valve gear.

In the Gooch gear, the throw of the eccentrics is usually made equal to half the full gear valve travel required, or very slightly more. The Gooch valve gear is easier to reverse than the Stephenson, as only the radius rod requires to be moved, whereas in the Stephenson gear, the expansion link and eccentric rods have to be raised and lowered, and the friction of the eccentric straps overcome.

The Allan "straight link valve" gear

In the Allan valve gear, both the expansion link and the radius rod are moved when reversing, but in opposite directions, and as the action is direct, die-slip does not amount to very much. This motion uses two eccentrics on the driving axle similar to the Stephenson and Gooch gears, the eccentric rods being coupled direct to the top and bottom of the expansion link. The radius rod carries a die-block working in the link slot, the weighshaft having two arms, one on each side, coupled to the radius rod and the link respectively. The weighshaft is often placed below the motion, the arm coupled to the expansion link being attached to the top pin of the link.

The respective lengths of the radius rod and eccentric rods are proportioned so that the arcs described by the radius rod and link are always tangential to each other. Thus the die-block will move in a straight line when the engine is reversed.

Either a box-type or an open type expansion link may be employed, the top eccentric rod pin being extended on each side so that the lifting links may clear both the link and the end of the radius rod. The radius rod should be made as long as possible if an accurate steam distribution is desired.

From the model engineer's point of view, the Allan valve gear is well worth consideration, the machining of the expansion link being somewhat easier than where a curved link is employed; but where space is limited and the radius rods and/or eccentric rods have to be on the short side, better results will be obtained by using the Stephenson gear with launch-type links and central suspension.

The Allan valve gear was used quite extensively in this country towards the end of the nineteenth century, a notable example being the famous Webb 2-4-0 Jumbos of the old London and North Western Railway.

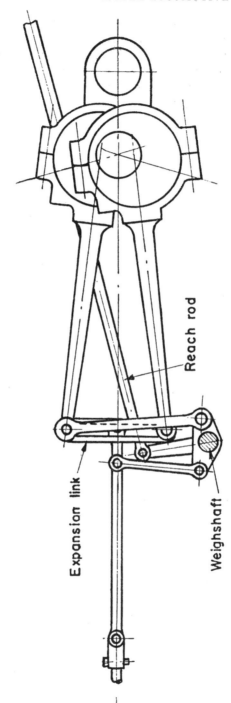

Reach rod

Expansion link

Weighshaft

Fig. 12   *Allan straight-link valve gear*

CHAPTER V

Radial valve gears (I)

THE RADIAL VALVE GEARS DIFFER FROM THE LINK MOTIONS IN THAT they partly or wholly dispense with the use of eccentrics. The best known are the Joy, the Hackworth, the Walschaerts and the Baker.

JOY VALVE GEAR

The Joy valve gear was introduced by David Joy in 1879, for locomotive, stationary and marine work. However, it is not at all certain that Joy was the inventor of this valve gear as A. Verey, a marine engineer of Dover, was using a similar gear at least ten years before this.

The Joy gear was extensively used in this country at one time, especially by the London and North Western Railway. It was mainly adopted for inside-cylinder locomotives, but has also been used for outside-cylinders. A good example of the latter application was the gear fitted to the narrow-gauge engines of the old Lynton and Barnstaple Railway.

The motion in Joy gear for inside cylinders is taken from the connecting rod through a system of levers, and no eccentrics at all are used. The connecting rod is constructed with an enlarged boss formed in it at a suitable point about one-third of the length of the rod from the small end. This boss is bored out and fitted with a bush through which a pin passes, projecting on either side to carrying the forked end of a lever known as the "correcting" link. The latter is coupled at its outer end to an "anchor" link which in turn is allowed to vibrate about a fixed point below the motion. This fixed point is generally a bracket attached to the motion plate; it may however be a frame stay or a shaft fixed across the frames, as is found most suitable for the particular engine.

The correcting link has a bearing in its central portion to which is connected the valve lever, usually named the vibrating lever. This is

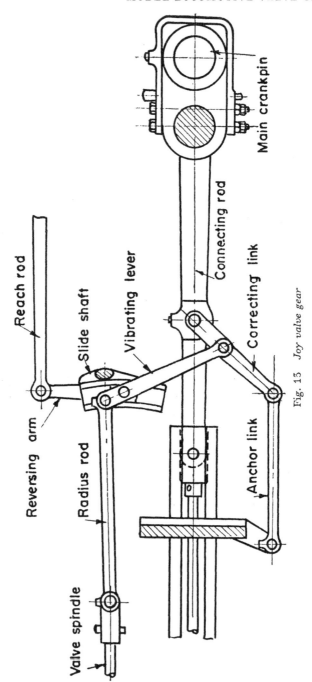

Fig. 15   *Joy valve gear*

further provided with two other bearings, one at the top end for the attachment of the valve rod, and the other close to it for a pin upon which work die-blocks, which are able to slide up and down curved guides attached to the weighshaft, these guides and weighshaft being collectively termed the slide-shaft.

It will be seen that the vibration of the connecting rod when the locomotive is in motion moves the die-blocks up and down in the slide-shaft, causing the valve rod to take a course depending upon the position of the guides. Thus when the slide-shaft is in a vertical position, the valve will have the least movement horizontally and the gear will be in mid gear. On movement of the weighshaft, the guides are tilted, the top end towards the cylinders for forward gear, and away from the cylinders for backward gear.

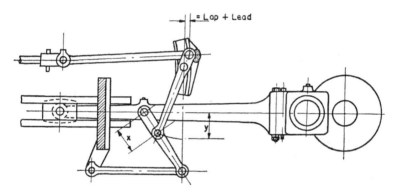

Fig. 14   *Setting out Joy valve gear*

In full-size practice, the Joy valve gear gave quite a good steam distribution where the valve travel was short, and the gear can be considered simple in construction and maintenance. The drilling of the connecting rod is perhaps a weak point in its design and this was in fact a source of trouble on some full-size engines, the connecting rods fracturing at this point. Another drawback to the Joy gear is the fact that it is affected by the up and down movement of the axleboxes in the horns. This latter drawback applies even more to a model locomotive, as miniature tracks are relatively rougher, and axlebox rise and fall relatively greater.

As no eccentrics are required with Joy's gear, it appeals to the model engineer, even though the slide-shaft, with its curved guides, is not an easy component to make. Where inside-cylinder locomotives for

$2\frac{1}{2}$ in. gauge and below are concerned, it will be found that there is very little width between the mainframes in which to accommodate the main cranks and the four eccentrics of Stephenson's or Gooch valve gear, due to the out-of-scale width of axleboxes, crankpins and crank webs etc., thus Joy's valve gear is often preferred.

Designing Joy valve gear

When designing a Joy valve gear for a model locomotive, the first thing to be decided is the full gear valve travel, and the dimensions of the valves and ports. The next point to be settled is the exact position on the connecting rod to locate the bush and pin for the correcting link. As mentioned previously, this position is generally about one third the length of the connecting rod measured from the small end.

The usual method of deciding the exact position is as follows: The motion is drawn out at least twice full-size, according to the scale of the model, the horizontal centre-line of the motion and the centre of the driving axle being drawn in. The connecting rod and crankpin are now drawn in four positions, the front and back dead-centre positions, and the positions where the connecting rod is at its highest and lowest position relative to the horizontal centre-line of the motion. It is now only necessary to locate the pinhole in the connecting rod such that its maximum movement in a vertical direction (vertical amplitude) is twice the full gear valve travel required, or very slightly more.

A vertical line should now be drawn at this position, and this locates the correct horizontal position for the weighshaft.

The length of the correcting link can now be decided. Its lower end, which is attached to the anchor link, must be sufficiently far away to allow of the angle between its two extreme positions being less than 90 deg.

The anchor link should be made as long as conveniently possible, so as to allow the end of the correcting link to rise and fall as nearly as possible in a vertical line. It is generally more convenient to fix the anchor link to a point forward of the connecting link.

To locate the correct position for the weighshaft in the vertical plane, the following procedure may be recommended. On the centre-line of the valve spindle, mark out vertical lines on either side of the vertical line previously drawn (when deciding the position for the pin in the connecting rod) at a distance from it equal to the required lap plus lead.

To take an example—if the required lap is ⅛ in., and the lead 0·025 in., then these lines will be 0·150 in. on either side of the original line, or 0·30 in. from each other.

Now assuming the crank to be upon its front dead centre, and the correcting link coupled to the anchor link, choose a point in the correcting link, which has for the moment to be assumed, rather nearer its upper pin than its lower pin. Draw a line representing the vibrating lever from this assumed point to the intersection of the rear vertical "lap and lead" line with the horizontal centre-line of the valve spindle; where this line crosses the central vertical line is the position for the weighshaft.

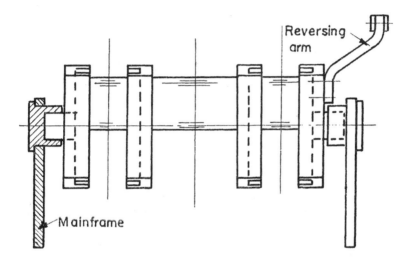

Fig. 15   *End elevation of Joy slide-shaft*

In practice the weighshaft is often placed a little higher than this, in order to give more clearance between the valve rod and the motion plate, and between the weighshaft and the central boss of the connecting rod. It should, where possible, be a little below the horizontal centre-line of the valve spindle.

The distance between the two upper pins in the vibrating lever is now also determined, as the upper pin is of course the point where the line representing the vibrating lever intersected the horizontal centre-line of the valve spindle.

The exact length of the vibrating lever is determined by the position of the central pin in the correcting link. This position must be such that when an arc the length of the vibrating lever is swung to the vertical centre-line (See Fig. 14) then x=y. In other words, the length of the vibrating lever is best determined by a simple process of trial and error on the drawing board.

It will be seen that the centre of oscillation of the die-blocks and the centre of the weighshaft trunnions exactly coincide with one another when the piston is at either end of its stroke. Thus it is possible to reverse the motion from full forward to full backward gear without giving any movement to the valve rod. Thus the lead is constant in all gears.

The radius rod in Joy gear should not be made too short, while the radius of the curved guides in the slide-shaft must of course be made equal to the length of the radius rod.

In full-size practice, as has been mentioned before, some locomotives fitted with the Joy valve gear experienced failure through the connecting rods bending or breaking. This is not likely to cause trouble in models, provided that plenty of metal is allowed around the boss in the middle of the connecting rod.

Construction of Joy slide-shafts

The only item of Joy's gear which might cause trouble in manufacture to the average model engineer is probably the slide-shaft.

One method of making the curved guides themselves is to clamp a suitable bar of steel to the lathe faceplate, its centre being arranged at a distance from the lathe centre equal to the radius required. A parting tool, ground with top rake and plenty of side clearance on both sides, is then set up crosswise in the lathe toolholder, at a distance out equal to the radius of the curved guides. Cutting should be carried out at the lowest speed available, a light depth of cut used, and plenty of cutting oil provided.

Another method, which generally produces a better finish, is to use an end-mill or slot-drill held in a milling spindle attached to the lathe top-slide or cross-slide, the back gear being engaged and the faceplate slowly rotated against the cutter. Alternately the end-mill could be held in the 3-jaw chuck or in a collet, and the blank for the curved guides held on a stout plate attached to the vertical slide, arranged facing the headstock. The blank is then rotated on a pin at the required radius.

When sufficient "channel" has been produced in this way to make the four sections of curved guides, these are cut off and cleaned up to size externally; they should also be polished on their working

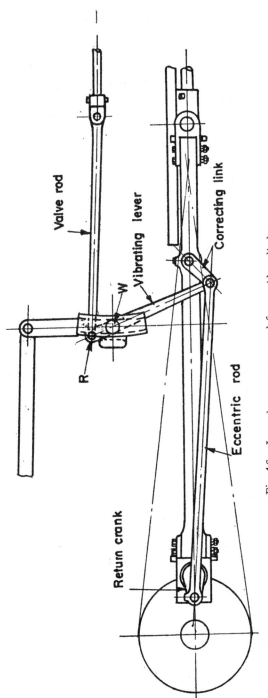

Valve rod

Vibrating lever

Correcting link

W

R

Eccentric rod

Retun crank

Fig. 16 *Joy valve gear arranged for outside cylinders*

surfaces. The weighshaft is then cut from rectangular steel bar and the four sections held to it by a small screw to each one. The sections are carefully lined up with one another and brazed to the weighshaft.

The reversing arm, which is attached to the driver's reach rod, is then fitted to one end, this usually being cranked outwards to bring the reach rod outside the mainframes, and the two trunnion pins, which work in bushes in the frames, are pressed home at either end. It is a good plan to make the overall length of the complete slide-shaft, measured over the trunnion pins, the same as the width between the mainframes, the trunnion bushes being put in from the outside and screwed to the frames. In this way, it is possible to slip the slide-shaft out from the frames, without having to disturb the frames themselves or any other components apart from the vibrating links and radius rods.

Joy valve gear for outside cylinders

The Joy valve gear has also been used for outside cylinders, though this application was never so common as the inside arrangement in full-size work. As it is not generally convenient to use an anchor link, attached to some fixed point on the mainframes, this link is dispensed with, and a short return crank is fitted to the main crankpin. This return crank is made approximately one third the length of the main crank, and arranged 180 deg. out of phase with it. Thus the return crankpin describes a circle of radius approximately two-thirds that of the main crankpin.

To this return crankpin is attached an eccentric rod, and the forward end of the eccentric rod is connected to another short link which works upon the pin in the connecting rod, as in the inside-cylinder arrangement of Joy's motion. The normal vibrating lever and slide-shaft are used, the bottom end of the vibrating lever being connected to the forward end of the eccentric rod, and to the link mentioned previously.

The Joy valve gear must be regarded as inferior to the Walschaerts' when used outside the locomotive, as the number of components and pins used is approximately the same as in the latter type of valve gear, while the Walschaerts' gear has the advantage that the lap and lead movement is quite separate from the eccentric or return crank drive to the radius rod, enabling a more accurate steam distribution to be obtained for both forward and reverse gear. On the other hand, the Joy motion may have an advantage on certain narrow-gauge type locomotives, where the driving wheels are very small, and the motion comes down very low and close to track level.

Designing Joy valve gear for outside cylinders is not quite as straightforward as the conventional inside gear. Fig. 17 shows, in three stages, how the design of the gear can be tackled. After drawing in the longitudinal centre-line of the motion and the line of the valve spindle, the connecting rod is drawn in four positions: at front dead-centre, at back dead-centre, and at the highest and lowest positions. The positions of the main crankpin and of the small end pin in the main crosshead are also drawn in, for these four positions of the connecting rod.

A point on the connecting rod, for the attachment of the correcting link, is now chosen such that its vertical amplitude is equal to $1\frac{3}{4}$ times the full gear valve travel desired, or a shade more. (distance x in stage one.)

The position of this correcting link pin is next marked for the four positions of the connecting rod described previously, that is points E.F.G.H. in stage two.

To determine the position of the weighshaft, a vertical line CD is drawn at 90 deg. to the horizontal centre-line of the motion and equidistant from the points E and F. The height of the weighshaft above the horizontal centre-line is generally determined by practical considerations, such as clearance for the connecting rod, proximity of the underside of the boiler, etc., but it may be placed a little below the horizontal centre-line of the valve spindle. (Point W in stage two.)

Lines are now drawn from points E and F at 45 deg. to the horizontal as shown. To determine the length of the correcting link EY and at the same time the length of the vibrating lever WY, a trial position of the point Y should be chosen, such that when the vibrating lever is swung to the vertical (on W as centre) it cuts the latter at such a position that the distance Z equals the length of the correcting link EY.

Having determined EY, the correcting link is now marked off for the back dead-centre position of the connecting rod, that is FT in stage two. The distance YT now gives us the required pitch circle of the return crank, that is, YT equals PC. The point J represents the position of the return crankpin when the connecting rod is at the front dead-centre position, thus JY gives the length of the eccentric rod.

The next stage is to determine the lap and lead functions. To do this, the vibrating lever is drawn in the two dead-centre positions, that is WY and WT, and this lever is then extended far enough above the weighshaft for the point R (to which the valve rod is attached) to

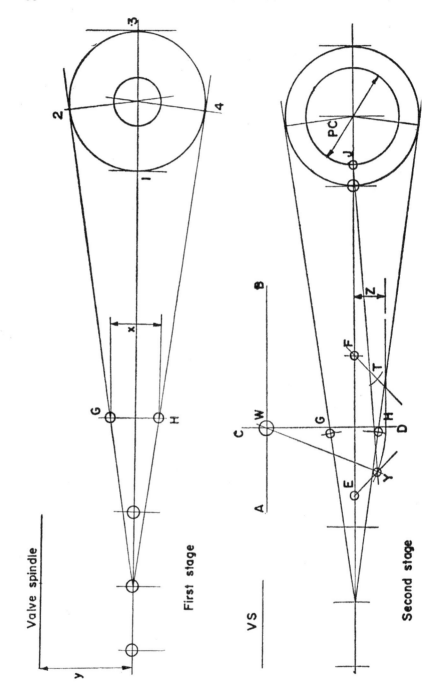

Valve spindle

First stage

Second stage

VS

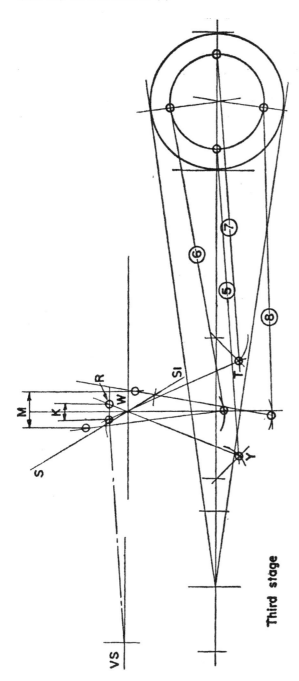

Fig. 17   Three stages in designing outside Joy gear

move through a horizontal distance equal to twice (lap plus lead), i.e. K in stage three.

The final problem is to determine to what angle, each side of the vertical, the slide-shaft must be rocked in order to produce the required full gear valve travel (M). This angle should be decided upon by a simple process of trial and error, by drawing in a line representing the slide-shaft (S–S.I.) and seeing to what position R is moved when the connecting rod is at its highest and lowest position respectively.

An important point to note is that the total angle of swing of the slide-shaft should never be more than 50 deg. (i.e. 25 deg. either side of vertical), otherwise there will be excessive friction in the slides. In the drawing (third stage) the angle of S–S.I. has been exaggerated to make the movements clearer.

If it should be found that even a total swing of 50 deg. does not give the desired full gear valve travel, then the only solution is to start at the beginning once again, and place the point of attachment of the correcting link on the connecting rod nearer to the big-end, i.e. increase the distance x in stage one. It must be remembered however that Joy gear is not an ideal valve gear for long valve travels. While the drawings given apply to cylinders with outside-admission slide valves, the instructions for determining the proportions of the valve gear apply equally well when piston valves are used except that the relative position of the main crankpin and valve crosshead are reversed by 180 deg., and the connections at the top of the vibrating lever are also reversed.

CHAPTER VI

Radial Valve gears (II)

HACKWORTH VALVE GEAR

THE HACKWORTH VALVE GEAR WAS INVENTED BY JOHN WESLEY HACK-worth in 1859. It is one in which the valve motion is taken from one eccentric, which is fixed on the driving axle exactly opposite the crankpin, and has its eccentric rod working vertically, the end of the eccentric rod being attached to a die-block which slides in a pair of straight guides.

These guides are pivoted, so that they can be turned to an angle to the vertical by means of the reversing rod. At a suitable point in the eccentric rod, a pin is provided for connecting the valve rod, the extreme end of which is attached to the valve spindle in the usual way.

When the guides are exactly vertical, i.e. the mid gear position, the valve rod connection is moved through an oval path, the horizontal amplitude of which is made equal to twice the lap plus lead. In full forward and backward gear, the guides are rotated sufficiently to increase this horizontal amplitude to the required full gear valve travel. With this gear, the lead is of course constant for all positions of the reversing lever.

The Hackworth valve gear is a comparatively easy one to make, and has few parts, but it cannot be recommended for model locomotives as unless the eccentric rod is made very short, trouble may be experienced in obtaining sufficient clearance for the guides underneath the boiler. At the same time, if the eccentric rod *is* made short, the valve events suffer. Another disadvantage of this gear is that the vertical movement of the axleboxes in the horns upsets the valve timing to some extent.

MARSHALL VALVE GEAR

The Marshall valve gear is a modified form of Hackworth gear, which was patented in 1879. A single eccentric is used, mounted on the driving axle, arranged in line with and on the same side of the

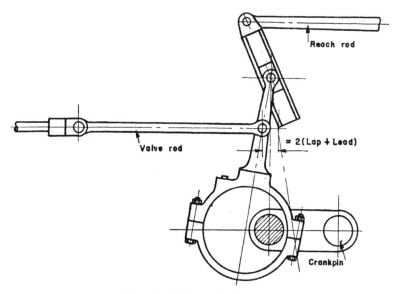

Fig. 18   *Hackworth valve gear*

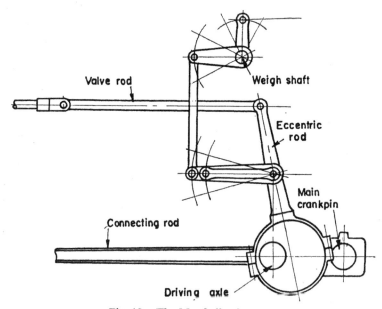

Fig. 19   *The Marshall valve gear*

Underside of a model Britannia chassis in ¾-inch scale.

A three-cylinder locomotive chassis in ¾-inch scale. All cylinders have separate Walschaerts' valve gears.

An overhead view of a 3-cylinder S.R. Schools class locomotive in ¾-inch scale.

Chassis of Schools class locomotive showing Walschaerts' valve gear *(bottom left)*.

Combination lever and valve spindle guides on model Britannia class locomotive.

axle as the crankpin. The eccentric rod has one pin at its end for connecting to the valve rod, and another between its extremities to which is connected a vibrating link. The opposite end of the vibrating link is attached to a pivoted lever which is moved by the reversing gear. Although the straight guides used in the Hackworth valve gear have been replaced in this gear by swinging links, the valve rod connection moves through an oval path similar to that produced by the Hackworth gear, and constant lead for all cut-offs is obtained, because the fulcrum of the vibrating link and the point of attachment of the valve rod connection to the eccentric rod coincide in both dead-centre positions. The drawing, Fig. 19, shows Marshall valve gear for operating outside-admission valves, and for inside-admission the eccentric centre must be moved in relation to the main crankpin through 180 deg., or the valve spindle may be connected to the eccentric rod between the eccentric and the vibrating link.

WALSCHAERTS' VALVE GEAR

The Walschaerts' valve gear, invented by M. Egide Walschaerts of the Belgian State Railway in 1844, is the most widely used locomotive valve gear at the present time, and is popular all over the world. If properly desinged, it is also one of the most efficient, while it can be used with equal effect outside or inside the locomotive frames.

The Walschaerts' gear is not, strictly speaking, a radial gear, as no ellipses are described by it. The travel of the valve is controlled by two quite separate movements, one being that of the crosshead, and the other that of an eccentric fixed upon the crank axle, or in the case of an outside-cylinder engine, a "return crank" fitted to the end of the driving crankpin.

Walschaerts' valve gear may differ a great deal in mechanical details, notably in the design of the expansion link, its suspension and the weighshaft arrangements. It may be required to operate valves with outside steam admission, or piston valves with inside admission; this necessitates a 180 deg. reversal of both the advance functions and the eccentric or return crank drive.

Where slide valves with outside admission are used, the vibrating or combination lever is arranged so that the valve spindle is attached to it above the radius rod connection, while with the normal position of the die-block—in the bottom of the expansion link for forward gear— the return crank is arranged effectively 90 deg. in advance of the main crankpin.

When inside admission piston valves are in use, the connections at

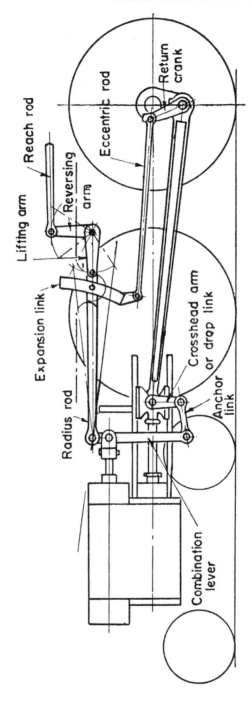

Fig. 20 *Walschaerts' valve gear for piston valve cylinders*

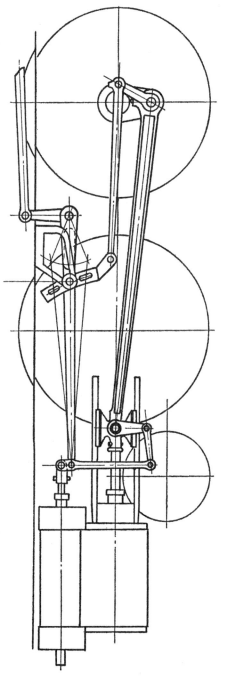

Fig. 21   *Walschaerts' valve gear for slide valve cylinders*

the top end of the combination lever are reversed, the radius rod connection being above the valve spindle, while the normal arrangement of expansion link necessitates the return crank being 90 deg. in retard of the main crankpin.

Before going further, it should be made clear that the return crank (or eccentric in the case of inside cylinders) is only arranged exactly 90 deg. in advance or retard of the main crankpin where the eccentric rod connection is an "all-square" one, i.e. the pin in the expansion link which takes the drive from the eccentric rod lies on the horizontal centre-line of the motion when in the middle of its travel.

Walschaerts' valve gear is most convenient when the valves are arranged above the cylinders, and the valve spindles offset to the outside of the engine. In the case of inside cylinders, the offset of the valve spindles is usually towards the centre of the locomotive. Average valve offsets for the different scales of model locomotives were discussed in Chapter 1.

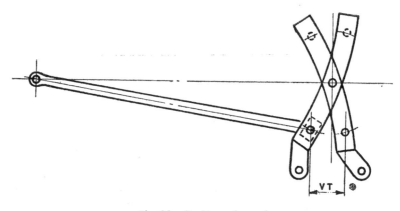

Fig. 22   *Radius rod travel*

Designing Walschaerts' valve gear for models

As with all other valve gears, the first things to be decided are the proportions of the valves and ports, and the full-gear valve travel to be adopted.

It was mentioned in previous chapters that large steam laps with long valve travels are recommended, though care must be taken to ensure that the valve travel required will not produce a valve gear that is mechanically impossible in the available space. The lead, being controlled by the combination lever, is constant at all positions of the reversing lever in Walschaerts' gear, and the amount of lead to allow was fully discussed in Chapter 1.

The total travel of the valve in full gear and for a normal full port opening is equal to the amount of the lap plus the port width multiplied by 2.

In Walschaerts' gear, the swing of the expansion link must not be made too great, or difficulty will be experienced in reversing the engine, through excessive friction of the die-block in the link. Generally speaking, the angle of swing should not be made more than 25 deg. to the vertical, i.e. a total swing of 50 deg.

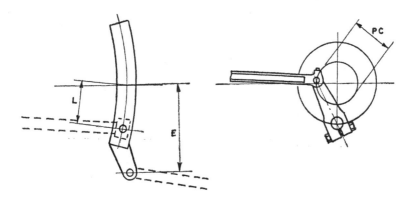

Fig. 23   *Determining the return crank pitch circle*

Expansion link Movement

Having decided the angle of swing of the expansion link, the effective length of this must be determined, in order to give the full gear valve travel desired. The effective length depends upon the length of the die-block, the radius of the link, and the swing of the link. It is best determined on the drawing board by drawing the link, to as large a scale as possible, in three positions: in its central or vertical position, in its maximum forward position, and in its maximum backward position. The length of the die-block can be made to an amount similar to that recommended for the die-block in Stephenson valve gear. From these three positions it is then quite simple to arrive at the clearances necessary, and thus what the effective length must be. In the diagram Fig. 22, the distance VT must be made equal to the

full gear valve travel, or very slightly more to allow for the inevitable
slight loss of motion in the pins and die-block.

The position for the eccentric rod connection is next settled, and
the pitch circle diameter of the return crankpin necessary to give the
desired movement. (See Fig. 23). For an inside cylinder locomotive,
where eccentrics are used in place of the return cranks, the dimensions are usually made almost equal, as if this was not done, the throw

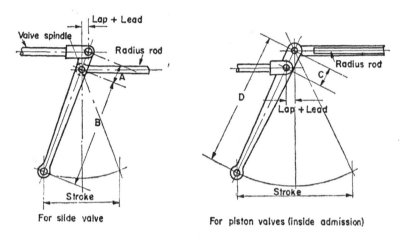

For slide valve   For piston valves (inside admission)

Fig. 24   *Setting out the combination lever*

required for the eccentrics would make these components unneces-
sarily large and cumbersome. The return crank pitch circle may now
be calculated as follows:

$$PC = \frac{VT \times E}{L}$$

The combination lever

The combination lever is operated by the main crank, its attachment
being usually made to the crosshead by a short link known as the
anchor or union link. In most British locomotives, owing to the length
of the combination lever in relation to the other components, it is
usual to employ an additional vertical link, fixed rigidly to the crosshead, in order to lower the rear end of the anchor link, and this
link is generally called the drop link.

The movement of the combination lever is 90 deg. out of phase with the movement obtained from the expansion link. Independently of the position of the reversing lever, the valve is moved by the combination lever to an amount equal to twice the lap plus lead.

The top joint proportions of the combination lever are now decided upon as shown in Fig. 24.

For slide valves:
$$\frac{A}{B} = \frac{2(Lap+Lead)}{Stroke}$$

For piston valves (internal admission):

$$\frac{C}{D} = \frac{2(Lap+Lead)}{Stroke}$$

If piston valves with outside admission are used, the formulae given for slide valves should be adopted.

The actual length of the combination lever is largely a matter of convenience, for if it is made too short, trouble may be experienced in arranging the top pins clear of one another. On some models, resort has been made to the use of cut-away pins, in order to get the top pins closer together, but if valves with reasonable lap and lead are specified this trouble will not arise.

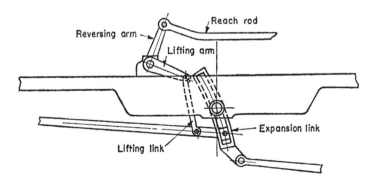

Fig. 25   *S.R. type expansion and lifting links*

When modelling prototype locomotives having the more modern piston valves with inside admission, if it is desired to use slide valves trouble will be experienced owing to the reversed connections at the top of the combination lever. If the radius rod was to be connected to the lower pin, and at the same time, the radius rod was to be arranged in the normal manner so as to lie parallel with the horizontal centre-line of the motion when in the mid gear position, it is almost certain that the expansion link and/or the lifting links would foul the connecting rod, and perhaps even the coupling rod. There are at least

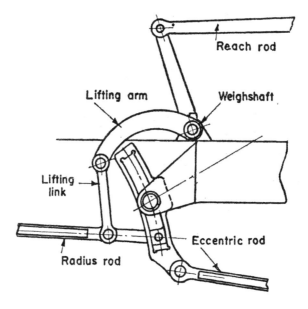

Fig. 26   *Forward-type lifting link*

three solutions to this problem: the valve crosshead may be offset vertically, so as to raise the combination lever and its connections. If this is done, the provision of some form of valve spindle guides should be considered. A second method is to arrange for the radius rod to be inclined downwards towards the combination lever, the original height of the expansion links and lifting links being maintained. This method cannot be recommended unless the radius rod is fairly long as slight errors in valve movement will be introduced, the valve events in back gear being different from forward gear for a given radial

Expansion link and lifting link of Britannia class loco-motive.

Walschaerts' valve gear on the Author's ¾-inch scale 2-6-4 tank engine.

An unusual arrangement of Baker gear on a 1-inch scale model locomotive.

Slip-eccentric gear fitted to the Author's gauge 1 4-4-0 locomotive.

Churchward-Stephenson gear fitted to the Author's 1-inch scale G.W.R. 2-6-2 tank engine.

Another view of the Churchward-Stephenson valve gear.

A necessary pre-requisite to good valve setting, "quartering" the driving wheels using the lathe and a dial test indicator.

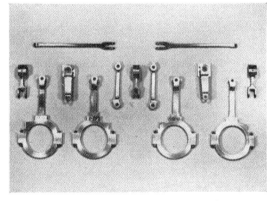

Some of the component parts of a Stephenson valve gear before assembly.

Lever reversing gear on a $\frac{3}{4}$-inch scale model.

setting of the lifting arms. A third solution is as used by the late Henry Greenly. A separate guide is employed, a die-block which works in this guide is then attached by a lug to the valve crosshead, while a pin through the middle of the die-block carries the front end bearing of the radius rod. While this method is thoroughly sound mechanically, its appearance may offend many model engineers.

Suspension of the expansion link

Wherever possible, Walschaerts' valve gear should be laid out so that all parts operate on centre-lines which are either parallel to

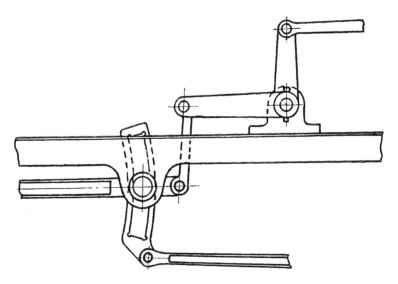

Fig. 27   *Lifting link on extended radius rod*

the horizontal centre-line of the motion or exactly at right angles to it.

The cylinders may be inclined, for various reasons, and this may have a slightly adverse effect on the valve movements due to excessive up and down movement of the driving axle, but it makes no difference to the setting out of the valve gear, the whole drawing may in fact be tilted to the required angle of the cylinders to simplify matters.

The horizontal position of the expansion link may now be decided upon, and this should if possible be arranged half-way between the driving axle and the valve spindle crosshead. This arrangement ensures

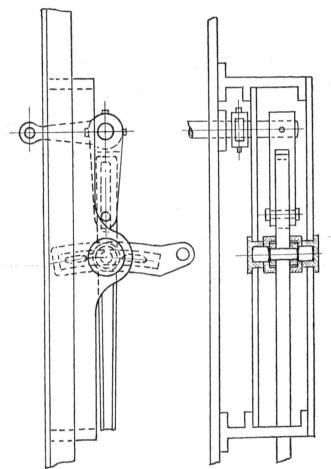

Fig. 28 *Link suspension in girder frame*

that both the radius rod and the eccentric rod are of reasonable length. The design of the casting or framework which supports the link varies in almost every class of locomotive. The L.N.E.R. used a steel casting which projected from the mainframes between the driving and coupled wheels and then forward again to a convenient point for the link bearings. The design of such a bracket should be gone into carefully as with many types of expansion link it is necessary to be able to assemble the link *in situ*, the outer support being placed into position after the expansion link itself.

Separate girder frames were often employed on the L.M.S., the frames spanning the space occupied by the driving and coupled wheels.

Walschaerts' valve gear should always be drawn out in plan and in end elevation as well as in side elevation to ensure that the necessary clearances are provided, particularly between the lower half of the expansion link and the connecting rod. The combination lever should be drawn at front and back dead-centres, to ensure that it clears the slide bars and

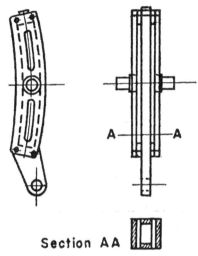

Section AA

Fig. 29   *L.N.E.R.-type   3-piece expansion link*

the boss of the crosshead, and does not foul the rear cylinder cover or packing gland when right forward.

Back-set of the expansion link

We come now to the design of the expansion link itself, and the determination of the correct amount of "back-set" for the eccentric rod pin in relation to the curved centre-line of the link slot. It is important that the expansion link should swing an equal amount on each side of its central position. Referring to Fig. 30 the theoretically correct arrangement is shown, but due to the angularity of the eccentric rod, this is not possible, and the pin in the "tail" of the expansion link must be set back sufficiently to counteract this angularity.

The effect of too much back-set is shown in Fig. 31, an unequal angle of swing being given to the expansion link. The correct solution is shown in Fig. 32. The amount of back-set is normally regarded as the distance of the eccentric rod pin in the link from the normal vertical centre-line of the link in the middle of its angular swing.

Although the correct amount of back-set can be calculated, it will be found easier to determine this by a simple process of trial and error on the drawing board. A pair of dividers may be used to determine the positions A, B, in the diagrams.

In some arrangements of Walschaerts' gear, notably in American locomotives, the "tail" of the expansion link is made longer, so that

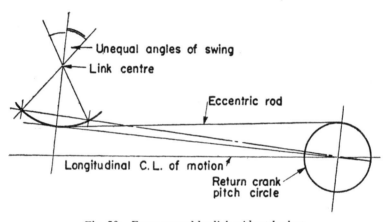

Fig. 30   *Error caused by link without backset*

the eccentric rod pin falls on the horizontal centre-line of the motion, giving an "all-square" layout. With this arrangement, the back-set appears greater than with the inclined connection more common to British locomotives.

The design of the expansion link

In some models, the expansion link is cut from plain mild steel plate of suitable thickness, and riveted or brazed to its trunnion pin, this pin being on one side of the link only, the radius rod with a single die-block lying on the other side. This scheme is quite satisfactory in small models provided the trunnion pin is of adequate length. An improvement would be to use "gauge plate" instead of mild steel.

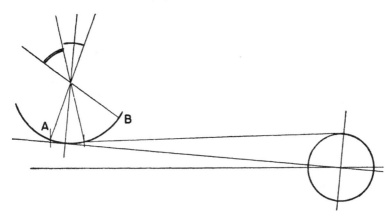

Fig. 31   *An excessive backset giving unequal angles of swing*

A better method for models over ½ in. scale is to arrange for a double bracket to be fitted to the link, each arm of the bracket carrying a trunnion pin, the radius rod is then forked to embrace the link itself. This method was used on many Southern Railway locomotives and is shown in Fig. 25. If this design is adopted, the lifting link should be made as long as possible to minimise die-slip.

Many railways had a preference for an arrangement whereby the radius rod is raised and lowered by means of a lifting arm behind the expansion link, and for this scheme the expansion link must be so designed that the radius rod can pass right through it. With this arrangement, there is very little die-slip in forward gear, and provided the presence of other coupled wheels does not interfere with the

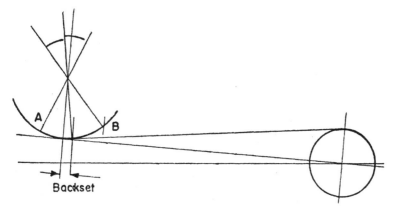

Fig. 32   *The correct backset giving equal angles of swing*

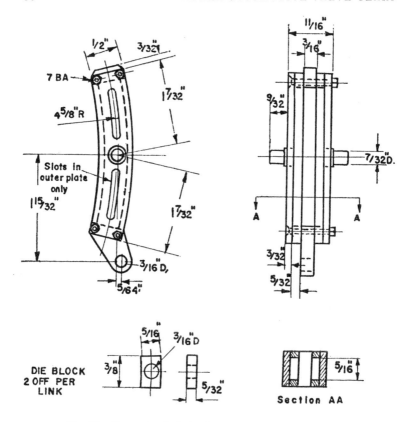

Fig. 33   *Expansion link for 1-in. scale L.M.S. locomotive*

weighshaft and its bearings, this is an excellent arrangement for a model as the weighshaft passes through the mainframes well below the bottom of the boiler, however low-pitched the latter may be.

The usual L.M.S. arrangement provided for a sliding type of lifting arm, the end of the radius rod beyond the expansion link being slotted and the end of the lifting arm carrying a rectangular die-block sliding in this slot. Fig. 33 shows the author's design for an expansion link of the L.M.S. type arranged for a 5 in. gauge engine. The "tail" of the link, or extension for the eccentric rod connection, and the top spacing piece are made of $\frac{3}{16}$ in. thick bright mild steel; the outer plates, which carry the trunnion pins, are of $\frac{3}{32}$ in. material, while the slotted plates are of $\frac{5}{32}$ in. steel, either mild steel case-hardened or gauge plate; the parts are held together by four 7 B.A. countersunk

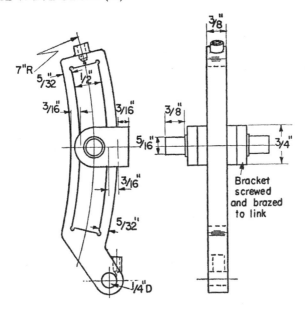

Fig. 34   *Another type of expansion link, dimensioned for* 1½ *in. scale*

steel screws so that the link can be assembled in position between the
link brackets. In this type of expansion link, the slotted plates can be
handfiled, the die-blocks being used as a gauge, or they may be milled,
as described in Chapter III.

On some ex-L.N.E.R. loco-
motives, the expansion link
was made in three pieces, the
radius rod being doubled
where it passes through the
link. Provided that the trunnion pins are arranged
exactly in line, this type of
link is very satisfactory and
not a difficult one to make,
the central slotted member
being milled or filed, while
its lower extremity carries
the pin for the eccentric rod
connection. The three-piece

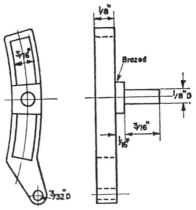

Fig. 35   *A simple type of expansion
link for* ½ *in. scale models*

link must also be designed so that it can be assembled *in situ*, as not only the outer link bracket member has to be attached after assembly, but the die-block must be put into position in the link slot, and the central member of the link slid into position between the two arms of the radius rod, before the link as a whole can be bolted up.

The return crank

The return crank is fixed to the outer end of the main crankpin, and with the die-block in the lower end of the expansion link for forward gear, is in advance of the crankpin for slide valve, external admission cylinders, or in retard for piston valve, inside admission cylinders. The angle of advance or retard must be exactly 90 deg. though this would only apply to an "all-square" layout. For an inclined layout, as used on most British locomotives, the angle of advance or retard will be more or less than 90 deg. by an amount corresponding to the inclination of the eccentric rod. It should be noted that there is a different length of return crank for a different return crank pitch circle, thus it is not possible to increase the valve travel of the valve gear concerned, merely by setting it farther out to describe a larger

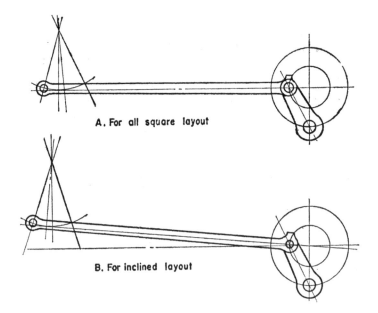

A. For all square layout

B. For inclined layout

Fig. 36   *Return crank setting*

pitch circle, a new return crank of the correct length would have to be made. See Fig. 36.

The fixing of the return crank is an important point in model locomotives, as there must be no possibility whatever of the crank shifting in service. A very good scheme for models of $\frac{1}{2}$ in. scale and above is to split the lower end of the return crank, a clamping bolt being put through this just clear of the crankpin. After the return crank has been correctly set, a standard taper pin of suitable size is put through the middle of both crankpin and crank. This method ensures that, should the return crank have to be dismantled at any time, it can be replaced in its correct position without any difficulty.

In full-size practice, the end of the main crankpin is sometimes squared, the return crank being clamped to this by a bolt immediately below the square; another method is to mill a slot across the face of the crankpin, the crank having a tongue to fit this for driving purposes, the securing being made by means of four set screws or studs. Neither of these methods can be recommended for model work, owing to the difficulty of obtaining the correct setting before machining either the end of the crankpin or the crank.

The setting of the return crank in its correct position on the crankpin can be done as follows:

The axleboxes are first jacked up to the designed running position, this is generally done by inserting small strips of metal of the required thickness between the bottom of each axlebox and the hornstays. The expansion link is now clamped in its mid position, that is a position such that the die-blocks can be run from top to bottom of the link without imparting any movement to the combination lever or valve spindle. The main crank is now set exactly on front dead-centre, while the return crank is set as near as possible by eye in order that its pin describes a circle of the diameter required by the design of the valve gear (PC in Fig. 23). With a pair of dividers, measure the distance from the centre of the hole in the tail of the expansion link to the centre of the return crankpin.

Now shift the main crank around to the back dead-centre position and offer up the dividers, without shifting them, as before. If they tally in this position, the return crank is correctly set, and can be bolted up and pinned; if the dividers do not tally the return crank should be shifted by half the amount of the difference. The same process should then be repeated, and it should be noted that when the dividers do tally in the two positions, they give the exact length required for the eccentric rod, which can then be made and fitted. Both sides of the locomotive should receive separate treatment as described above, owing to the possibility of slight differences in dimensions.

In recent years, miniature ball bearings and needle roller bearings have been used with success for the eccentric rod return crankpin bearings of larger models. If ball bearings are used, these may be of the self-aligning type. Needle roller bearings make a neat eccentric rod big end, but for this type of bearing both the pin and the eccentric

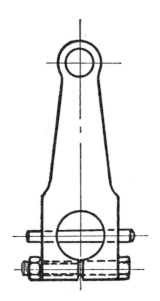

Fig. 37 *A good method of fixing return cranks*

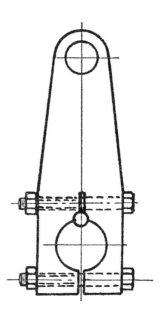

Fig. 38 *Another method of fixing return cranks*

rod itself must be hardened. For models of $1\frac{1}{2}$ in. scale and above, twin-row ball races or proper roller bearings could be considered. Such bearings generally have a much longer life than the more usual gunmetal bushes, especially if fitted with proper dust-excluding caps as in full-size practice.

The making of valve gear parts such as eccentric rods, radius rods, combination levers, etc., may sometimes appear rather laborious, especially in the larger scales, owing to the large amount of metal which has to be removed between the bearings. In large components, much time can be saved, in the absence of a regular milling machine, by first filing out a gap wide enough to allow a hacksaw blade to be inserted. After sawing, the component is finished by milling, the rod being clamped in a machine vice mounted on the vertical slide in the lathe. Short levers may be dealt with in a similar way, the holes being of course drilled first, when the lever can be held down on a stout steel bar, the bar being bolted to the vertical slide, and an end-mill used in the collet or self-centring chuck.

The circular type of boss at the ends of components can often be finished quite neatly by swinging them bodily on a pin against an end-mill revolving in the lathe. The pin required can be turned on the end of a piece of square bar, which is then clamped under the lathe tool-holder parallel to the lathe mandrel. When using this method, great care should be taken to move the work in the opposite direction to the cutting teeth, otherwise the end-mill may catch up and ruin the component. A similar method has been used, where a suitable grinding wheel replaces the end-mill in the former operation; here again care must be taken, and the cut applied kept to the minimum possible.

The pin-holes of as many valve gear components as possible should be bushed with a good-quality bearing metal such as phosphor-bronze, but if this is not possible owing to the small size of the bearing, the eye of the component can be case-hardened and polished.

Before leaving the Walschaerts' valve gear, it is perhaps worth mentioning that the method of arriving at the full-gear valve travel just described, although a sound practical one, is not absolutely accurate. The actual valve travel produced is modified by the angular movement of the combination lever, and of course it also depends upon the distance between the two upper pins and the lower pin in the combination lever.

To arrive at the exact longitudinal amplitude of the pin connecting the radius rod to the combination lever we can use the following simple formulae:

For internal admission cylinders

$$\text{Long. amplitude of pin} = 2\left(\frac{R\sqrt{v^2-l^2}}{R-l}\right)$$

For external admission

$$\text{Long. amplitude} = 2\left(\frac{R\sqrt{v^2-l^2}}{R+l}\right)$$

where R = radius of main crank (half stroke of engine).
v = half the full gear valve travel.
l = lap plus lead.

THE BAKER VALVE GEAR

This valve gear, invented by Abner D. Baker of Ohio, U.S.A. in 1903, is a modified form of the Walschaerts' motion wherein the expansion link is replaced by a system of cranks and levers. For a time it was popular in America, and in some other countries, but was never employed on British Railways.

The return crank is arranged to give considerably more throw than is usual in Walschaerts' gear, and it drives an eccentric rod which is connected to a lever known as the gear-connecting rod. This lever is in turn connected at its top end to a bell crank which drives the valve rod. The gear-connecting rod is pivoted to another lever known as the radius bar, which is itself pivoted to the reversing yoke.

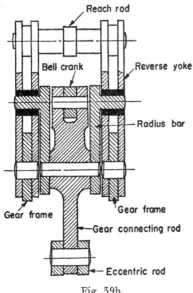

As can be seen in the end section, Fig. 39b, the reverse yoke is generally doubled, and pivots at its lower end on the gear frame, which is bolted to the mainframe of the loco-motive.

The fulcrum point of the gear-connecting rod can thus be moved from its neutral position —in line with the radius bar— to a position either side of it, giving an angular movement to the bell crank and thus a longitudinal movement to the valve rod.

The Baker valve gear has always enjoyed a certain popu-larity with the model engineer, chiefly owing to the fact that no expansion link, with its curved guides and die-blocks, is required. It is also comparatively easy to fit up, the necessary levers being attached to the gear frame which can be bolted to the mainframe in a suitable position by angles. In the larger scales, all the pins in Baker gear can work in bronze bushes, so that these can be quickly removed and re-placed when wear takes place. It is however important that all pins in this gear are carefully fitted, otherwise there will be considerable lost motion with a corresponding bad effect on the valve timing.

Fig. 39b.

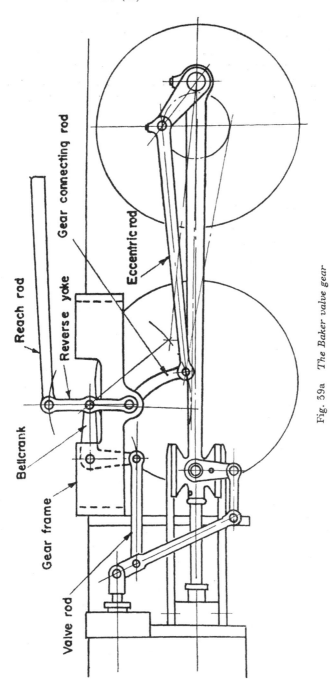

Reach rod

Gear connecting rod

Reverse yoke

Eccentric rod

Bellcrank

Gear frame

Valve rod

Fig. 39a   *The Baker valve gear*

In comparing the Baker gear with the Walschaerts' gear, it must be remembered that although there is no expansion link or die-block, and therefore no die-slip, on the other hand there are a large number of pins, upon which wear takes place; and especially when the eccentric rod is short, the return crank carries a considerable load. In Baker gear, the eccentric rod should, whenever possible, be made at least 5 times the return crank pitch circle. In locomotive designs where a short eccentric rod cannot be avoided, a smoother working will be obtained by the use of Walschaerts' valve gear.

Designing Baker valve gear for models

The author has been unable to find, in any of the model engineering manuals, textbooks, or journals, any reference to designing Baker gear for any particular model locomotive, and as a result, the model engineer has had to resort very largely to the unwise practice of trying to adapt an existing design to his own particular case, relying on adjustments to the return crank to increase or decrease the full gear valve travel.

In view of this, the following hints on laying out Baker valve gear may be found useful.

The full gear valve travel should of course be settled in advance, as previously described, as should the lap and lead, the latter being dealt with by the combination lever in exactly the same way as for Walschaerts' gear.

The horizontal centre-line of the motion, the cylinders, the centre-line of the valve spindle, and the shape of the mainframes, also the bottom line of the boiler should now be drawn out, to as large a scale as possible. The centres of the driving and coupled wheels and their outside diameters should then be added, clearance being allowed for the rise and fall of the wheels in the horns.

Coming now to the reverse yoke, radius bar and bell crank, the horizontal position of these items should be such that the eccentric rod can be of reasonable length, at the expense even of the valve rod. The valve rod in Baker gear does not need to be relatively as long as the radius rod in Walschaerts' gear.

The distance between the pins in the reverse yoke and radius bar are to a large extent settled by the proportions of the model itself, as already drawn—i.e., the vertical distance between the horizontal centre-line of the motion and the valve spindle, the distance from the former to the top line of the mainframes, and the distance between

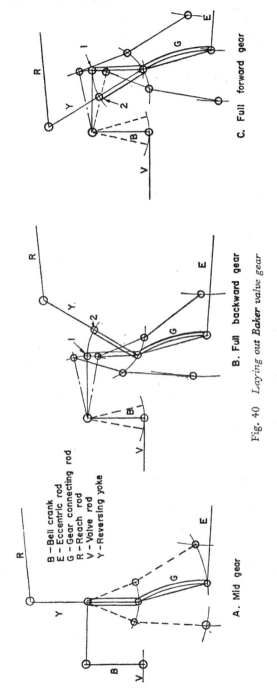

B —Bell crank
E — Eccentric rod
G — Gear connecting rod
R — Reach rod
V — Valve rod
Y — Reversing yoke

A. Mid gear

B. Full backward gear

C. Full forward gear

Fig. 40 *Laying out Baker valve gear*

there and the underside of the boiler. In the case of American proto-types, there is usually ample room to allow these components being made of reasonable proportions.

A further examination of the gear will now show that the full gear valve travel obtained depends mainly on the following four factors: the proportions of the bell crank, the angular swing of the reverse yoke, the pitch circle described by the return crankpin, and the distance between the bottom pin of the gear connecting rod and its central pin (relative of course to its effective overall length).

The swing of the reverse yoke should not be made more than about 25 deg. either side of the vertical, i.e. a total swing of 50 deg.

As regards the bell crank, although this is generally made with equal arms, there is no objection to the vertical arm being made longer than the horizontal arm, up to a ratio of about 5:4. In this way the full gear valve travel can be increased quite considerably without the introduction of appreciable errors. A further point to note is that with internal admission cylinders, the lower pinhole of the bell crank may lie considerably lower than the corresponding front pin-hole of the valve rod (i.e. where the valve rod is connected to the combination lever); even with slide valves, there is no objection to this within reason. This will be found to assist design, as it allows of more clearance between the front end of the gear frame and the valve rod itself, without any likelihood of the bell crank fouling any other part of the motion.

Coming to the length of the gear connecting rod, the bottom pin-hole of this rod should not fall below the horizontal centre-line of the motion, in fact it may lie some distance above it, as is the case in Walschaerts' gear on most British locomotives.

Having determined suitable proportions for the bell crank, re-verse yoke, and gear connecting rod, and their situation on the frames in relation to cylinders and driving axle, etc., the final work to be done is to decide upon the return crank pitch circle to give the de-sired full gear valve travel. Fig. 40 shows a suitable graphic method. The upper and lower positions of the horizontal arm of the bell crank form the key to the situation. Having drawn in the position of the reverse yoke for full forward gear and full backward gear respectively, it will be seen that the middle pin of the gear connecting rod can only move on the arc described with "2" (Fig. 40) as centre. As the longitudinal amplitude of the bottom pinhole of the gear connecting rod is at this stage still an unknown quantity it will be seen that there are two ways of determining the extreme forward and extreme backward positions of this rod. The amplitude can for the moment be assumed, and trial positions drawn in until the pinholes coincide as required, or a simple model of the rod may be made up and applied to the drawing board. If the latter method is adopted (though this may not appeal to skilled draughtsmen) a suitable model rod can be cut out very quickly from thin tinplate or even cardboard, and the three pinholes accurately drilled or pricked through. The top pinhole is then located on the pinhole in the horizontal arm of the bell crank, and the middle hole located on the arc previously mentioned; thus the three positions as seen in Fig. 40 for the eccentric rod connection may be obtained, and the return crank pitch circle decided upon.

THE JONES' VALVE GEAR

The Jones valve gear is a modified form of Walschaerts' gear, having the feature of variable lead. An additional link having a curved slot is connected to the reversing arm and slides between fixed guides. The sliding die-block is restrained from horizontal movement by a guide link pivoted to the mainframes of the locomotive, and is connected to the top of the combination lever by a link whose centre is fixed to the radius rod. When the reversing gear is moved, the die-block in the normal expansion link and the additional link are both moved at the same time, resulting in a variable lead which increases to a maximum in mid gear.

THE BEAMES' VALVE GEAR

The Beames valve gear is a modification of Walschaerts' gear in which the valves of inside cylinders are operated by an outside motion. This valve gear was introduced to avoid troubles that were experienced on certain locomotives fitted with Joy gear, mainly failures of connecting rods carrying an intermediate bearing for operating the valve gear.

The lower end of the combination lever is oscillated by a rod connected to a forward extension of the coupling rod. The combination lever is suspended from a guide bar supported in a bracket fitted to the outside of the mainframe of the locomotive. This bracket also carries a pivoted lever working through a slot in the frame. The

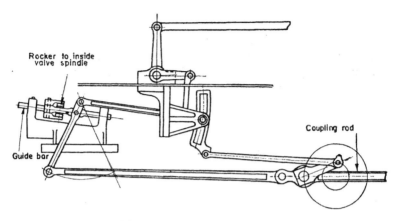

Fig. 41   *The Beames valve gear*

outer end of this pivoted lever is connected to the guide bar and its
inner end to the valve spindle of the inside cylinder. The return
crank, expansion link, and reversing arrangements are arranged as in
a normal Walschaerts' valve gear.

GREENLY'S CORRECTED MOTION

Greenly's Corrected Motion, which can be used for both inside
and outside cylinders, is based on the Joy gear, but uses a slide-shaft
with straight slides. It was devised by the late Henry Greenly and has
been used on a number of model locomotives with success.

The straight slides of the slide-shaft are easier to machine than
the curved slides in the Joy gear; they can be milled from the solid
by means of a face cutter, or they could be end-milled. In the larger
scales, they could be built up from steel sections without any machining being done at all. This valve gear allows the use of pins of adequate
size and is suitable for engines where the pitch of the boiler is not
too low, owing to the space required for the slide-shaft. As far as
prototype British locomotives with outside cylinders are concerned,
this motion may be ruled out on the score of appearance, but it is well
worth consideration for inside-cylindered locomotives.

In the Greenly Corrected Motion, the motion is derived from a
point on the connecting rod below and immediately in front of the

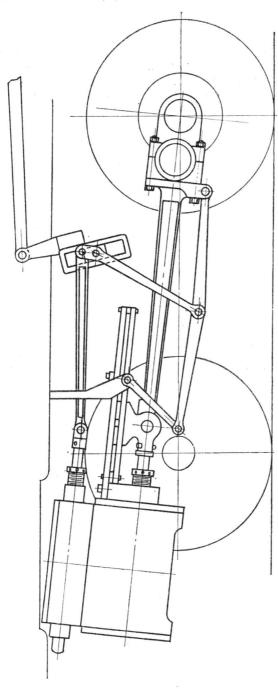

Fig. 42   Greenly "corrected" valve gear for inside cylinders

big end bearing. At this point, a swinging link is attached by means of a lug. A substantial pin may be fitted here. The other end of this swinging link is supported by a correcting link which is pivoted from some convenient fixed point on the chassis or from a lug attached to the motion plate. From a point roughly half-way along the swinging link is attached the lower end of the vibrating lever, which is shaped as in Joy's gear. The two upper pins in the vibrating lever are situated close together and control the lap and lead functions. With the normal external admission slide valves the top pin is connected direct to the valve rod, the pin just below it to the die-blocks. With internal admission piston valves, these two pins are reversed, the upper pin being arranged through the die-blocks.

The function of the correcting link is not only to carry the front end of the swinging link, but to lift it at each dead-centre to the exact amount required to neutralise the loss in height of the vibrating lever due to the angularity of the latter in these two positions.

The setting out of this motion should be done to as large a scale as possible, so that the necessary clearance for the various links may be allowed. The pivot point on the connecting rod should be decided upon first, then a point on the swinging link should be chosen that will lift the die-block sufficiently to open the valve fully to steam when the slide-shaft is inclined to not more than 25 deg. from the normal vertical position. With the big end on dead-centre, and the vibrating lever swung to its farthest extent, a line should be drawn in representing the swinging link, and farther along this link a point should be chosen for the attachment of the correcting link. The length and pivot point of this is chosen so that in swinging the lower end shall lift to coincide with the vertical movement of the bottom pin of the vibrating lever.

With a long valve rod, the steam distribution of this gear compares favourably with the standard Joy valve gear.

CHAPTER VII

Valve gears for three- and four-cylinder engines

MANY FOUR CYLINDER LOCOMOTIVES USE ONLY TWO SETS OF VALVE
gear to operate all four valve spindles. Where the two outside cranks
are set at 90 deg. to one another and adjacent outside/inside cylinders
at 180 deg. to one another, two sets of valve gear may be used with no
more complication than a simple rocking lever having a fixed pivot
approximately at its centre. The valve gears may be outside the frames,
as in the ex-L.M.S. Pacific locomotives, or inside the frames as in the
ex-G.W.R. Stars, Castles, and Kings. In the latter classes of engine,
inside Walschaerts' valve gear is used, the radius rods being forked

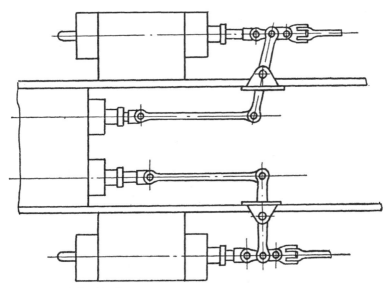

Fig. 43   *Four-cylinder engine: outside to inside gear*

71

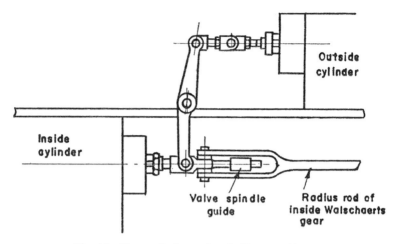

Fig. 44   *Four-cylinder engine: inside to outside gear*

to clear the inside valve spindles and their guides, while a bent lever connects the inside valve spindles to the outside via a differential screw.

An interesting type of valve gear was at first fitted to the pioneer 4-cylinder express locomotive of the old Great Western Railway, No. 40 *North Star*, designed by the great G. J. Churchward. In this engine, the valve gear was fitted between the frames, yet no eccentrics were used. The combination levers, as in the normal Walschaerts' arrangement, were driven by the main crossheads. The levers to operate the expansion links however were derived from the opposite inside crossheads by means of a reducing linkage. This was possible because the main cranks of the leading coupled axle were at 90 deg. to one another; and the gear became known as the Scissors valve gear.

Although it proved quite satisfactory in service, the Scissors gear was dropped in favour of the normal Walschaerts' arrangement in the later Star class engines. It is said that this was because of a protest received by the Great Western from the Midland Railway. Apparently Swindon was accused of making use of the Deeley valve gear without acknowledgement. Mr. R. M. Deeley, of the Midland Railway, designed a valve gear very similar to that fitted to No. 40, and in 1905 fitted it to the famous No. 990, a 4-4-0 type express engine. However neither Deeley nor Churchward were really first in the field as regards this type of valve gear, for the valve gears originated earlier by Stevart in Belgium, and by Lewis and Young in the U.S.A. were

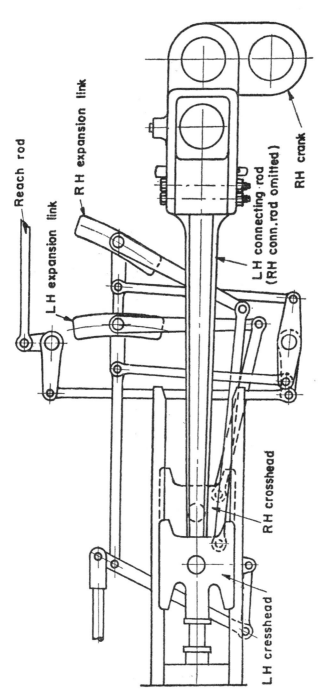

Reach rod

R H expansion link

L H expansion link

RH crank

L H connecting rod
(RH conn. rod omitted)

R H crosshead

L H cresshead

Fig. 45   *Deeley cross-drive valve gear*

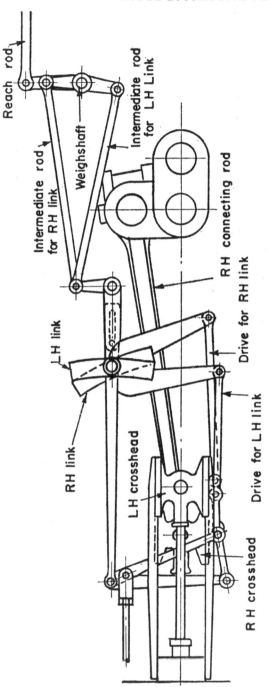

Fig. 46 *Churchward's "scissors" valve gear*

Lining up the expansion link brackets: Walschaerts' gear

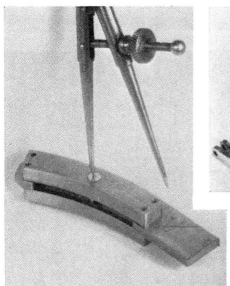

Marking out the eccentric rod pinhole: Walschaerts' gear.

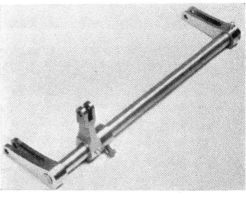

Walschaerts' gear: weigh-shaft fitted with lifting and reversing arms.

Milling flute in eccentric rod using lathe and vertical slide.

Milling flute in connecting rod using small horizontal milling machine.

examples of cross-connected valve gears with their movement derived from main cranks at 90 deg. to one another.

For four-cylinder locomotives with the cranks set at 135 deg. (giving eight impulses per revolution of the driving wheels) Mr. H. Holcroft has shown how the two inside valve spindles can be operated by a conjugated motion derived from the movement of the two outside valve spindles. Three levers are used, one being fully floating, and the other two pivoted to the frames of the locomotive. In the diagram Fig. 47, the outside right-hand crank is set 90 deg. from the outside left, the inside left-hand crank is set 45 deg. from the outside right, the inside right-hand crank is set 90 deg. from the inside left, and the outside left 135 deg. from the inside right. In the circle shown, a line

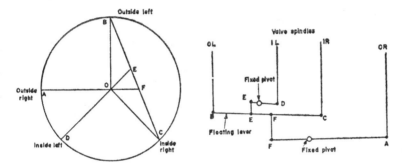

Fig. 47   *Diagram of Holcroft arrangement for 4-cylinder engine, cranks at 135 deg.*

is drawn connecting the O/L to the I/R. Another line is drawn from the O/R through the centre of the circle to cut the line O/L–I/R at F, and another line is drawn from the I/L through the centre to cut the line O/L–I/R at E. The valve motion consists of a rocking lever AOF attached to the outside right-hand spindle at A, pivoted to the frame at O, and attached to the floating lever (BEFC) at F. The floating lever is attached to the outside left-hand valve spindle at B and to the inside right spindle at C. The other rocking lever DOE is attached to the inside left spindle at D, pivots on the frame at O, and connects to the floating lever at E.

The proportions of the three levers can be taken from the diagram, but may of course be made of any length to suit the spacing of the valve spindles of the locomotive concerned, provided that the correct proportions are maintained.

Conjugated motion for three-cylinder locomotives

Conjugated motions for operating the valves of the inside cylinder by means of levers connected to the two outside cylinders of a three-cylinder locomotive were devised by the late Sir Nigel Gresley and by Mr. H. Holcroft. The well-known Gresley gear utilises a long lever having a fixed pivot and a short floating lever. The former is made with its pin-holes spaced in the proportion 2:1, while the floating lever is made 1:1. The cranks of the engine must be set at 120 deg.,

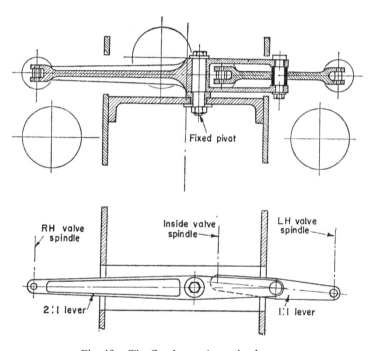

Fig. 48   *The Gresley conjugated valve gear*

although if the inside cylinder is inclined at a different angle to the outside cylinders, allowance for this difference must be made when adjusting the driving wheels on the crank axle. The Gresley gear was used on a very large number of ex-L.N.E.R. locomotives with great success, but when the standard of locomotive maintenance fell, as happened during the 1939–1945 war, the conjugation was not quite so effective owing to the cumulative effect of lost motion in the various pins.

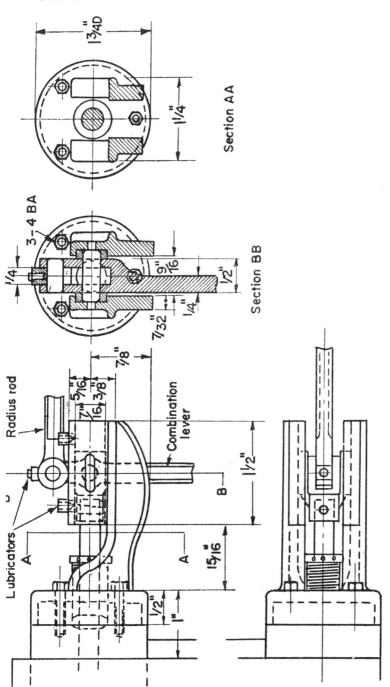

Fig. 49   *Arrangement of valve spindle guide and top joints for a 7¼ in. gauge engine with Walschaerts' gear*

On most of the L.N.E.R. locomotives, the valve spindles of the outside cylinders were extended beyond the front of the cylinders so that a connection could be made to the two-to-one levers. With this arrangement, the expansion of the outside cylinder valve spindles had to be allowed for, but on the 4-4-0 Shire and Hunt classes, and the 4-6-0 Sandringham class, the connections were made at the rear of the cylinders, so this trouble did not arise.

While this valve gear is quite satisfactory in model work, it is important that the cranks be correctly set, and that there be no appreciable lost motion in the various pins. The outside valve gears too must be accurately set, otherwise the valve events of the inside cylinder will suffer.

CHAPTER VIII

Poppet valve gears

POPPET VALVES FOR STEAM LOCOMOTIVES WERE FIRST TRIED IN THE early part of the nineteenth century, but they were introduced much before their time as neither the materials nor the manufacturing skills then available were sufficiently good for the purpose. It was not until 1906 that they were successfully adopted in locomotives.

The poppet valve differs from the slide valve and piston valve in its method of opening, for it is moved bodily away from its seating during the time steam is passing through it; it also remains stationary during the time it is closed. Another difference is that separate valves are generally used for steam admission and exhaust, thus four valves are required for a normal double-acting cylinder.

Poppet valves used in full-size locomotives are always of the double-beat type, that is they have two distinct seating faces joined together by a cylindrical portion. This has the important advantage over the single seat type that the area through the valve for a given lift is nearly doubled. It also greatly reduces the force required to open the valve, as it is nearly in balance.

Poppet valve gears may be divided into two main classes, oscillating and rotary. The former are fitted with cams which oscillate through about one quarter of a revolution and are operated by an ordinary link or radial type of valve gear. The latter have cams which receive a rotary movement either directly or indirectly from the driving axle, generally through gears.

The reversing and "notching-up" of the gears is obtained, in the case of the oscillating cams, the same way as for a piston valve or slide valve engine, but in the rotary gears, this is obtained by altering the angular position of the cams relative to the main crank.

Very few model steam locomotives have been built with poppet valve gears of any type, no doubt due to the extra complication involved, not only in the valve gear, but also in the cylinder.

The oscillating cam gear and the rotary cam gear with horizontal

79

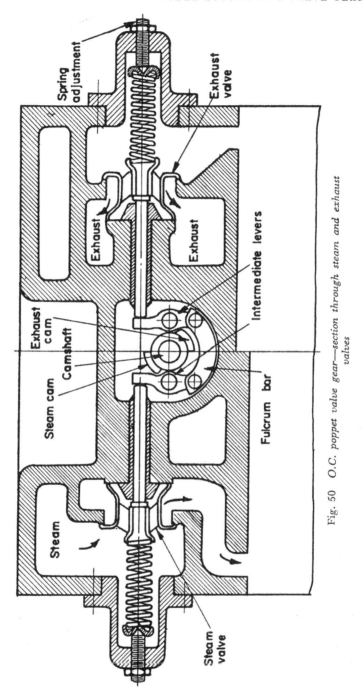

Fig. 50 *O.C. poppet valve gear—section through steam and exhaust valves*

valves are probably the easier to build in model form, the author therefore proposes to deal with these two types in some detail in the hope that these notes will be of help to experimentally-inclined model engineers. The drawings are intended primarily to make the working clear, details of construction are not elaborated.

Oscillating cam gear

In the oscillating cam poppet valve gear, the most commonly used arrangement is that with horizontal side-by-side valves. There are two steam valves, one for each end of the cylinder, arranged above the cylinder itself and towards the outside. The two exhaust valves are situated side by side with the steam valves, closer to the main-frames. All the valves open away from the centre of the cylinder block, and are closed by means of compression springs provided with external adjustment.

The live steam is generally admitted from above to each end of the steam chest by means of the usual outside steam pipe. The exhaust steam passes towards the centre of the cylinder block in two separate passages. These arrangements can be seen in Fig. 50.

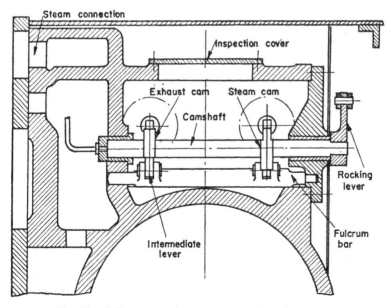

Fig. 51   *O.C. poppet valve gear: section through camshaft*

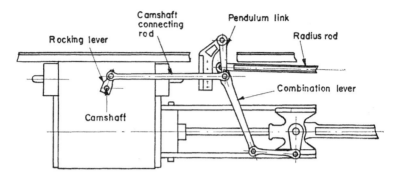

Fig. 52   *O.C. poppet valve gear: arrangement of drive*

The cams are mounted on the camshaft so that their profiles are opposite each other. Levers are interposed between the cams and the inner end of each valve spindle, carrying rollers midway between these two to make contact with the cams on the horizontal centre-line of the camshaft. The lower ends of the intermediate levers are pivoted on a fulcrum bar which is rigidly secured to the cylinder casting by an outer cam cover. The complete cam mechanism is arranged so that it can be withdrawn from the cylinder as a unit with the cam cover.

On the outside end of the camshaft is mounted a short rocking lever which is connected to the camshaft connecting rod. This rod takes the place of the valve rod in conventional gears, thus if Walschaerts' gear is being used this rod is connected to the top of the combination lever immediately below the radius rod. A pendulum link is generally provided so that guides are not required.

The valve setting of this type of poppet valve gear can be divided into two sections. The first is the adjustment of the length of the valve spindles and the adjustment of the return spring tension; the second is the synchronisation of the cam gear. The correct valve spindle length is such that there is reasonable clearance between the inner end of the spindle and the appropriate intermediate lever, with the raised part of the cam clear of the roller fitted to the intermediate lever. In this position the valve will of course be hard upon its seating.

To enable the valve spindle lengths to be checked, preferably while hot, owing to the expansion of the various parts, an inspection cover should be provided immediately above the camshaft.

To synchronise the camshaft, the camshaft rocking lever is placed in the vertical position, the engine crosshead at mid-stroke, and the reversing gear in the mid gear position. A temporary camshaft connecting rod is then erected and its length adjusted to suit the distance between the camshaft rocking lever and the pendulum link.

Another method of operating a poppet valve gear of the oscillating type is by the Lentz variable-eccentric drive.

A rotary drive is obtained by mounting a gearbox on the driving axle or upon a return crank the centre of which coincides with the centre of the driving axle. A shaft is arranged across the engine and behind the cylinders, having a gearbox at one end connected to the return crank gearbox by a shaft fitted with universal joints. The cross-shaft receives a rotary motion in the same direction and at the same speed as the driving axle.

At the gearbox end of the cross-shaft are splines which engage the driven gear, thus the shaft is not only rotated but can be moved laterally. This lateral movement is controlled by a toothed rack which engages with a gear wheel connected to the cab reversing gear.

The cross-shaft has oblique projections on it which engage with slots in a bar fixed in the centre of an eccentric, while the eccentric

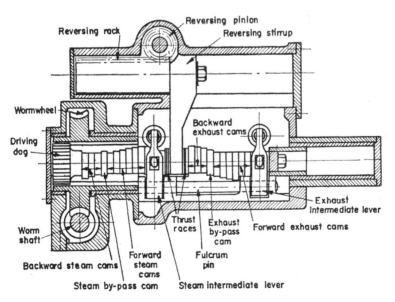

Fig. 53 *Sectional elevation of "rotary-cam" cam box*

rod is connected to the camshaft rocking lever. As the reversing gear is operated, the cross-shaft is moved laterally causing the eccentric centre to be varied, giving the usual variation in cut-off in each direction.

Rotary cam gear—horizontal valves

The cylinders and valves for this type of gear are generally similar to those used with the oscillating cam gear previously described.

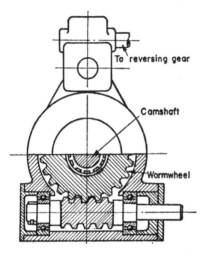

In place of the single cam for each pair of valves, however, a number of equally-spaced cams are provided for controlling the steam valves and for the exhaust valves, although more cams are usually provided for forward than for backward gear. Between the forward and backward gear cams there is a neutral or by-pass cam to hold the valves stationary in the open position. The profile of each cam is chamfered off into the adjacent one so that as the camshaft is moved laterally to alter the cut-off or to reverse the engine, the rollers on the intermediate levers move easily over the cams.

Fig. 54   *Cross-section through driving shaft: rotary-cam gear*

The cams are arranged on the camshaft so that the full forward gear profiles for both steam and exhaust are at the same end of their respective sets of cams while the full backward gear cams are similarly arranged but at the opposite end of their respective sets.

Between the sets of steam and exhaust cams is a thrust box and engaging with this is a stirrup fixed to a reversing rack above and in line with the camshaft. This rack can be moved laterally by a pinion fixed to the reversing shaft so that rotation of this shaft moves the camshaft, thus altering the cut-off or reversing the locomotive as required.

The steam and exhaust intermediate levers, the fulcrum pins, and the rollers which make contact with the cams are all arranged as in the oscillating cam gear previously described except that the rollers have their corners chamfered off to facilitate their movement as the camshaft is moved laterally.

The centres of both the steam and exhaust rollers must be in line with the centres of their respective cam profiles for all rates of cut-off; when notching-up, the camshaft is moved in graduated steps, equal to the centre distance between the cam profiles; thus some indication must be provided on the reversing gear so that the driver's handle is moved the correct amount to bring the cam required exactly in line with the rollers.

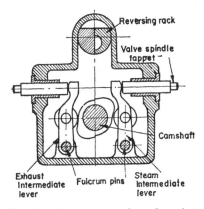

As regards the rotation of the camshaft, this is usually provided for by means of a driving dog having keys engaging with keyways in the driving shank which carries a wormwheel.

Fig. 55   *Cross-section through valve tappets: rotary-cam gear*

This wormwheel is turned by a multiple-start worm driven from a return-crank gearbox at engine speed, by means of a universally-jointed shaft.

CAPROTTI VALVE GEAR

The Caprotti valve gear, evolved by A. Caprotti of Milan in 1921, employs vertical poppet valves operated by rotating cams, and was produced with the idea of improving the thermo-dynamic performance of the steam locomotive.

The chief disadvantages of normal valve gears are centred in the fact that when an early cut-off is used, the corresponding points of release and of compression are similarly advanced. An early cut-off is obtained and the point at which the exhaust port opens is also early. This causes restrictions in the length of the expansion curve and the pressure at the moment of exhaust is higher than it would be were the point of release delayed. Further, since the point of compression is also advanced, in order to run at early cut-offs, it is necessary to employ larger clearance volumes to prevent excessive compression at the end of the stroke and larger clearance volumes mean a greater consumption of steam.

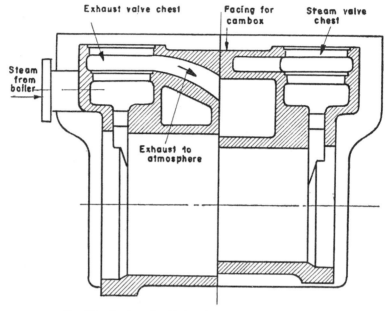

Fig. 56   *Section of cylinder for Caprotti poppet valves*

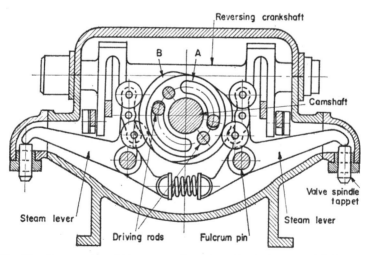

Fig. 57   *Cross-section of Caprotti cambox (through inlet levers in full forward gear)*

The Caprotti system, by employing separate means for operating the steam and exhaust valves, makes it possible to maintain the periods of release and compression constant for any degree of cut-off. Thus the two advantages are secured of obtaining more work from the expansion of the steam and obtaining a reduction in clearance volume. These points together result in a considerable improvement in the efficiency with which the steam is used in the cylinders. In full-size locomotives, the Caprotti gear has an additional advantage over other gears in that there is a reduction in frictional losses.

Each cylinder is provided with four valves, two live steam and two exhaust, working in a vertical plane, the steam valves being arranged nearest to the frames. Each valve operates in a separate cage having integral seatings for the top and bottom faces of the valve, between which are ports for allowing the steam to pass into and out of the cylinder. The valves are arranged above the cylinder barrel and are pushed downwards to open, the seatings being above the valve faces. All the valves are mounted on spindles working in bushes fixed to the valve cages.

The valves are lifted up to their seatings by means of live steam admitted by the regulator, thus when the latter is closed, the valves fall away and thus establish communication between the two sides of the piston, so effecting a by-pass to allow free running of the engine.

The cams for controlling the valve movements are mounted so that they can be turned by a revolving shaft driven from the driving axle at engine speed. Three cams are used for operating the four valves of each cylinder. Two cams, A and B in Figs. 57 to 59 control the steam valves, and one, C, the exhaust valve.

A crankshaft, D, cross-connected to its opposite number on the other cylinder, and connected by gearing to the driver's reversing handwheel, is arranged at right-angles to the camshaft as shown in the plan view, Fig. 59. This crankshaft by means of links E is coupled

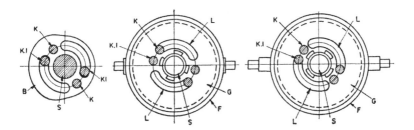

Fig. 58 *Caprotti cams and cam rods*

to two sleeves, F, which are very similar to eccentric straps. These sleeves embrace cylindrical sheaves G1 and G2 which are threaded to work on a quick-pitch screw, H, formed on the revolving camshaft S.

The two steam cams are located nearest to the crankshaft D, and the exhaust cam is located at the outer end, away from the crankshaft. The cams are loosely mounted on the camshaft but they are given a rotary motion by means of cam rods K and K1, which are driven by the sheaves engaging on the quick-pitch screw.

Slots L, cut in the sheaves, allow the direction of motion and the function of the cams to be reversed, the sheaves again taking over control when they have been turned through a sufficient angle.

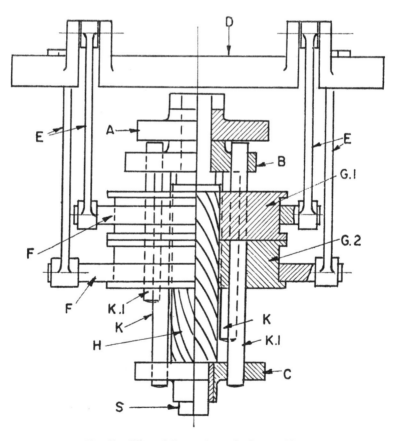

Fig. 59   *Plan of Caprotti camshaft assembly*

It will be noticed that the valves are actuated by bell cranks; the ends of the inlet bell cranks next to the cams are fitted with equal arm levers carrying rollers bearing on the two steam cams. When running in the direction of the arrow shown, the cam A is acting as the admission cam for the valve on the left-hand side, which has been opened, while the cam B is acting as the cut-off cam.

When the engine is reversed, the links E move the sleeves F and thus the sheaves G1, G2 along the screw, rotating them and therefore having the effect of reversing the functions of the two steam cams.

The position of the exhaust cam relative to the valve operating levers is not altered in so far as the time of the opening and closing of the valves is concerned, until the reversing gear is in the mid gear position. Thus the points of release and compression remain the same whatever amount of cut-off is employed.

The Caprotti system has been applied to three- and four-cylinder locomotives as well as two-cylinder. A well-known example of the four-cylinder type was the ex-Great Central 4-6-0 Lord Faringdon class, now withdrawn, while the solitary British Railways' class 8 Pacific *Duke of Gloucester* is a fine example of the three-cylinder engine.

In the *Duke of Gloucester*, the drive for the camboxes of the outside cylinders is taken from the driving axle by means of worm-gearboxes mounted on return cranks. Tubular shafts transmit the drive from the gearboxes to the camboxes. The drive for the cambox of the inside cylinder is taken from an extension on the worm-shaft on the left-hand cambox through a right-angle bevel gearbox.

COSSART VALVE GEAR

As the Cossart valve gear requires a supply of compressed air to lift the valves against the action of the closing springs, it cannot be regarded as an ideal type of motion for even the largest working model. However if air brakes were fitted to the locomotive, it might be feasible to use a proportion of the compressed air from this source, the air being taken from the reservoir.

The general design of the cylinders used in a Cossart gear resembles that used with the Caprotti gear. The valves are similar to normal poppet valves but are provided with grooves into which spring rings are fitted to take the place of the poppet valve seats. These valves work in liners into which ports are cut for the passage of the steam.

Each valve liner has two sets of ports, one for steam through the

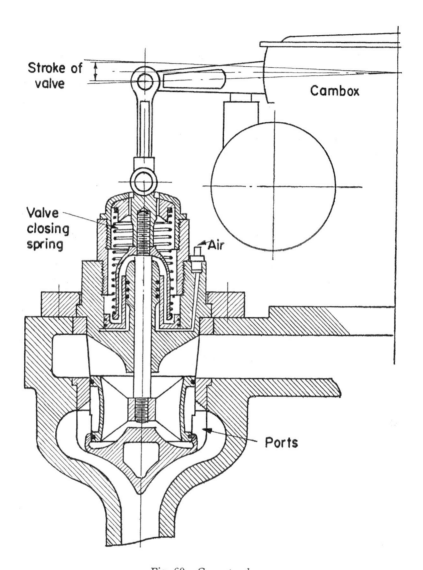

Fig. 60   *Cossart valve*

STAGES IN CONSTRUCTING ECCENTRIC RODS:

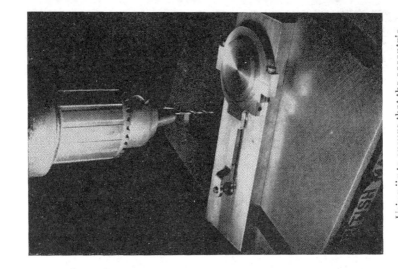

Using jig to ensure that the eccentric rods are of equal length.

Boring the eccentric strap.

Facing side of an eccentric strap.

End-milling link slot in the lathe. →

→ A view of the link blank showing the special milling attachment made by the Author.

Finished expansion links for Stephenson valve gear.

inside of the valve and the other for steam round the outside of the valve. As the valves are lifted, they uncover the ports in a similar manner to the piston valve, and their movement is the reverse of that of the valves in the Caprotti gear. Each valve is provided with a stout compression spring to ensure it being returned to the down or closed position against the pressure of the steam. Air pressure from the Westinghouse brake system fitted to the locomotive is used to overcome this spring and lift the valve to provide a free by-pass. This air pressure is controlled by a valve coupled to the regulator, so that every time the regulator is shut, all the valves are opened.

The reversing gear is cam operated and the valve operating cams have double profiles and rotate at half engine speed. One admission cam serves as the opening member and the other as the closing member in either direction of running. One cam only is used for the exhaust valve, thus the release and compression events are constant for all cut-offs.

To obtain the rotary motion necessary for the cams, a return crank and rocking beam are fitted to each side of the engine. The return cranks are fitted to the engine cranks and the rocking beams are pivoted on the frames about half-way between the cylinders and the driving axle.

The lower end of each rocking beam is connected by a balanced rod to its respective return crank, and the upper end to balanced cranks secured to the auxiliary driving shafts by spring-loaded rods. The auxiliary driving shafts are connected across the engine by a further shaft so that by the combined movements of the return cranks, the cams are rotated in the opposite direction to the driving axle.

This gear gives a constant lead, release and compression with an infinite variation of cut-off for forward and backward gears.

CHAPTER IX

Cab reversing gear, valve setting and the indicator

THE CAB REVERSING GEAR OF MOST FULL-SIZE LOCOMOTIVES IS OF THE screw type, though some goods and shunting engines use a long lever attached direct to the bridle or reach rod. As operating the reversing gear on many locomotives proved an arduous task for the driver, coming on top of all his other duties, some railway companies provided power reversing, either by the use of steam from the boiler or by using compressed air from the Westinghouse brake system.

In model locomotive practice, the screw type is easier and quicker to make and gives a finer adjustment of cut-off. However where the engine may be required to work upon an up-and-down line, the hand lever is often preferred.

The whole reversing gear should be made quite rigid, the stand should be of stout material bolted direct to the mainframes wherever possible. The stand is sometimes riveted to the frames, but this construction cannot be recommended, as it may prove necessary, at a later stage of the building of the locomotive, or during a major overhaul, to remove it altogether. In most types of locomotive, it is usually essential to offset the longitudinal centre-line of the reversing gear away from the frame so as to bring the lever or screw nearer to the adjacent cab side and clear of the backhead fittings. This can be accomplished by putting a "set" in the stand, or by using a thick spacing piece between frame and stand.

Where a screw reverse is used, the nut itself must be a good fit on the thread and may be made of gunmetal or phos/bronze, the screw being cut from a good-quality steel, a left-hand thread being preferable. The nut can be arranged to slide in guides to prevent any rocking motion being imparted to it.

The choice of left- or right-hand drive is usually influenced by the arrangement on the full-size engine, but if the hand-lever type of reversing is selected, it will be found easier to operate, at least in the smaller scales, if put on the left.

The reach rod, if made to scale dimensions, will probably whip quite considerably; it should therefore be made of fairly heavy section, and can be of greater depth towards its centre. On large locomotives over $1\frac{1}{4}$ in. scale, an intermediate guide or support may be provided

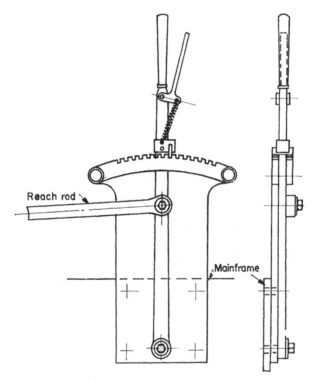

Fig. 61   *Lever reversing gear*

with advantage, about half-way along its length, allowance being made for the rocking movement of the reversing arm and lever.

The locating of the notches in the lever type of reversing gear may be done by moving the reversing lever forward very slowly, while turning the wheels in a forward direction. When the position of the lever is such that the valves are receiving their designed full gear travel, the lever is clamped, and the position for the forward full gear notch marked out. At the same time, it is very important to check

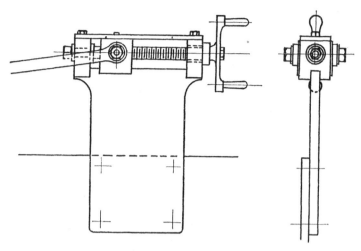

Fig. 62   *Screw reversing gear*

that in this position the die-block of the valve gear does not foul the end of the slot in the expansion link, or, in the case of a Joy valve gear, the die-block does not run out beyond the end of its curved guides.

The operation can now be repeated for backward gear, and the position for the full backward gear notch marked out. For the mid gear position, the lever is moved to such a position that no longitudinal movement is given to the radius rod by the expansion link (for a Walschaert's type gear). Where Stephenson gear is used, the lever is moved to such a position that the movement of the valve rod or intermediate valve rod, or for that matter, the valve spindle itself is at a minimum. The location of the intermediate notches on the sector plate can then be marked out between the full and mid gear notches as convenient.

Valve setting

Some mention was made of valve setting when dealing with the Stephenson valve gear. The purpose of valve setting is to get the valve events as close to the theoretical movements as possible, to equalise as near as possible the steam distribution for the front and back ports, and to correct any errors that may have crept in during the making and erecting of the valve gear. In general it may be said that there are two distinct methods of valve setting; one is to set the valves to give equal leads for front and back ports, the other is to set the valves to give equal openings for each port in full gear or at a cut-off near to full gear. The former is undoubtedly the better method when dealing with locomotives with valve gears giving constant lead. The latter may be used where the gear gives variable lead, according to the amount of cut-off.

Using the equal lead method, the full-gear valve travel should be checked, then the lead at each dead-centre compared. The dead-centre must be obtained with care as the valves travel rapidly when opening. If there is any difference in the leads obtained in different

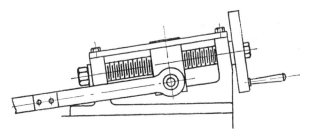

Fig. 63   *Another type of screw reversing gear*

positions of the reversing gear, a compromise should be effected, the most accurate setting being chosen at that cut-off likely to be most used in regular forward running.

The Indicator diagram

The indicator provides a graphic record of what is accomplished by the steam in the cylinder. The indicator is connected by specially drilled holes to the clearance spaces at each end of the cylinder. The pressure in the cylinder at any given moment is allowed to act upon a small piston, which forms part of the indicator, and transmits its movements through a system of levers to a recording pencil and drum.

Each indicator diagram shows the distribution of the steam at one end of the cylinder during one revolution.

Fig. 64 shows an ideal steam distribution diagram for a piston moving in the direction of the arrow. The straight line at the bottom is the atmospheric line which is drawn before the steam enters the cylinder. Directly the steam is admitted at A, the pencil goes up to B, which is the highest pressure reached in the cylinder. The valve now closes again, at C, at which point the steam is cut off. From B to C therefore represents the period of admission.

After steam has been cut off, there is a gradual pressure drop, and this is the period of expansion which ends at D, the point of release, when the exhaust is opened. At this point the pressure drops rapidly and then remains close to the atmospheric line until the piston reaches E. The exhaust then closes, compression begins, and pressure rises until the valve once again opens to steam at A.

The indicator diagram shows clearly the economy effected by working at early cut-offs. The diagram will also expose inefficient steam

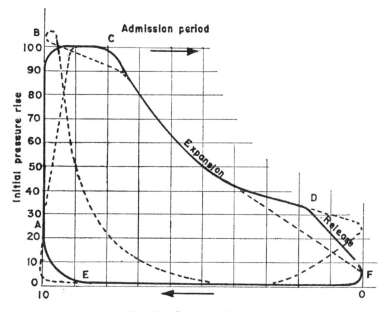

Fig. 64   *Indicator diagram*

distribution or a faulty valve setting. Such defects are shown in Fig. 64 by a dotted line. A sloping admission line from A to B shows a delay in the opening of the valve, as the piston would have moved a short distance before the full pressure had become effective. If the valve had opened too early, the same line would slope in the other direction.

A line falling from B to C would indicate a throttling of the steam during the admission period. If release takes place too early in the stroke, the line would fall away just before the point D, while if release is too late in the stroke the expansion line would be continued too far towards the end of the stroke and the correct amount of back pressure would not be attained until the piston had moved some distance on its return journey.

A too early closing of the exhaust causes excessive compression which could in some cases exceed steamchest pressure, causing a loop in the diagram at B. If the exhaust valve closes too late, a sharp bend will appear in the line between E and A, compression being insufficient.

The indicator diagram can also be used to compute the amount of work performed in the cylinders. The indicated horse-power is obtained by multiplying the mean effective pressure (obtained from the diagram) in pounds per square in., by the area of the piston in square in., by the speed of the piston in feet per minute, and dividing the product by 33,000.

In full-size locomotive work, the Dobbie–McInnes and the Crosby indicators are most commonly used. The Dobbie–McInnes indicator uses two indicating cylinders fitted with pistons and parallel motions and receiving steam from both ends of the cylinders. The pressure springs are arranged outside the steam cylinders, and two recording pencils are used, working on the same drum. By means of a cord attached to some moving part of the engine, the drum is moved at each stroke of the pistons.

In the New Crosby indicator, the piston is spherical in shape and is connected to the pencil mechanism by a rod ending in a ball and socket joint in the centre of the piston.

There seems to be no reason why indicators should not be made and used on model locomotives as small as 1 in. scale. The mechanism would have to be designed so that as little steam as possible was drawn from the cylinder in operating the pencil. The pencil actuating mechanism would also have to be very lightly but accurately constructed.

Fittings such as these offer yet further means of increasing the efficiency of model locomotives, and would provide endless fields of experimental work for the true steam enthusiast.

THE CHOICE OF A VALVE GEAR

Before completing this short work, the author would like to add a few notes on the choice of a valve gear for any particular model locomotive.

On first consideration, it might be thought that the choice of the valve gear to be fitted would be an obvious one, in that the valve gear adopted on the full-size prototype engine should be automatically adopted for the model. This is not necessarily so however. For instance,

in model locomotives below ¾ in. scale with inside cylinders, it is not
at all easy to fit Stephenson, Gooch or Allan valve gear owing to lack
of space between the frames to accommodate the four eccentrics
necessary, plus the main cranks.

In a case like this, the adoption of Walschaerts' or Joy gear may be
considered, the former requiring only two eccentrics for the two
cylinders, while the latter valve gear dispenses with the use of eccentrics altogether.

Another case which sometimes arises is one in which the prototype
uses perhaps a type of valve gear which does not appeal to the builder.
For instance, some model locomotive enthusiasts appear to have a
definite preference for Walschaerts' gear over Stephenson's, and where
inside cylinder locomotives are concerned, there is generally little
difficulty in such an alternation of design, unless the valves are arranged
between the bores of the cylinders. Such an alteration, being
entirely between frames, would not of course spoil the "scale"
appearance of the locomotive.

Some locomotive builders, constructing say a modern Pacific type
of engine, prefer to fit Baker valve gear rather than the Walschaerts'
gear usually found on British Pacifics, in order to avoid having to
make the curved expansion links required for the latter valve gear.
Such an alteration will not meet with the approval of the more
expert model engineer, who generally considers that a more sensible
course would be to build a purely free-lance type of locomotive;
however all tastes must be catered for!

Finally we come to the genuine free-lance model, and here the
choice of the valve gear to be used will obviously rest entirely on the
opinion of the designer. For those who are possibly for the first time
designing their own locomotive, a great point is accessibility, and it
is here that such gears as Walschaerts' and Baker's score, the former
having in addition a most attractive motion to watch, especially at
low speeds.

In conclusion let us remember that there is no such thing as the
best valve gear. One type of valve gear may suit a particular style of
locomotive better than another for a variety of reasons, many of
which have been discussed in previous chapters; and most readers
will agree that herein lies much of the fascination of the steam
railway locomotive, whether full-size or model.